WITHDRAWN

NEW ACCENTS

General Editor: TERENCE HAWKES

Deconstruction:

Theory and Practice

IN THE SAME SERIES

*Not available from Routledge, Chapman and Hall, Inc. in the USA

Deconstruction: Theory and Practice

CHRISTOPHER NORRIS

ROUTLEDGE
London and New York

First published in 1982 by
Methuen & Co. Ltd
Reprinted five times
Reprinted 1986 with a revised bibliography
Reprinted twice in 1988
by Routledge
11 New Fetter Lane, London EC4P 4EE
29 West 35th Street, New York, NY 10001

Printed in Great Britain by
Richard Clay Ltd, Bungay, Suffolk

British Library Cataloguing in Publication
Data
Norris, Christopher
Deconstruction.—(New accents)
1. Semiotics and literature
I. Title   II. Series
801'.95   PN98.S46.

Library of Congress Cataloging in Publication
Data
Norris, Christopher.
Deconstruction, theory and practice.

(New accents)
Bibliography: p.
Includes index.
1. Deconstruction. I. Title. II. Series:
New accents (Methuen)
PN98.D43N6   801'.95   81-22422

ISBN 0-415-03982-7 (pbk.)   AACR2

Contents

General Editor's Preface

It is easy to see that we are living in a time of rapid and radical social change. It is much less easy to grasp the fact that such change will inevitably affect the nature of those academic disciplines that both reflect our society and help to shape it.

Yet this is nowhere more apparent than in the central field of what may, in general terms, be called literary studies. Here, among large numbers of students at all levels of education, the erosion of the assumptions and presuppositions that support the literary disciplines in their conventional form has proved fundamental. Modes and categories inherited from the past no longer seem to fit the reality experienced by a new generation.

New Accents is intended as a positive response to the initiative offered by such a situation. Each volume in the series will seek to encourage rather than resist the process of change, to stretch rather than reinforce the boundaries that currently define literature and its academic study.

Some important areas of interest immediately present themselves. In various parts of the world, new methods of analysis have been developed whose conclusions reveal the limitations of the Anglo-American outlook we inherit. New concepts of literary forms and modes have been proposed; new notions of the nature of literature itself and of how it communicates are current; new views of literature's role in relation to society flourish. *New Accents* will aim to expound and comment upon the most notable of these.

In the broad field of the study of human communication, more and more emphasis has been placed upon the nature and function of the new electronic media. *New Accents* will try to identify and discuss the challenge these offer to our traditional modes of critical response.

The same interest in communication suggests that the series should also concern itself with those wider anthropological and sociological areas of investigation which have begun to involve scrutiny of the nature of art itself and of its relation to our whole way of life. And this will ultimately require attention to be focused on some of those activities which in our society have hitherto been excluded from the prestigious realms of Culture. The disturbing realignment of values involved and the disconcerting nature of the pressures that work·to bring it about both constitute areas that *New Accents* will seek to explore.

Finally, as its title suggests, one aspect of *New Accents* will be firmly located in contemporary approaches to language, and a continuing concern of the series will be to examine the extent to which relevant branches of linguistic studies can illuminate specific literary areas. The volumes with this particular interest will nevertheless presume no prior technical knowledge on the part of their readers, and will aim to rehearse the linguistics appropriate to the matter in hand, rather than to embark on general theoretical matters.

Each volume in the series will attempt an objective exposition of significant developments in its field up to the present as well as an account of its author's own views of the matter. Each will culminate in an informative bibliography as a guide to further study. And, while each will be primarily concerned with matters relevant to its own specific interests, we can hope that a kind of conversation will be heard to develop between them: one whose accents may perhaps suggest the distinctive discourse of the future.

TERENCE HAWKES

Acknowledgements

My thanks to all those in Cardiff, especially Catherine Belsey, Rachel Hollis and Richard Machin, whose readiness to talk and criticize has seen me through some awkward patches. Also to Terence Hawkes, the onlie begetter, for his tireless editorial guidance and sustaining interest. My debts nearer home are very partially repaid by dedicating this book to my wife Alison and the illustrated, pop-up edition to my daughter Clare. I am grateful to the editors of *The Journal of Literary Semantics*, *Essays in Criticism*, *Poetry Nation Review* and *The British Journal of Aesthetics* for permission to reprint portions of articles that have appeared in their pages.

Introduction

> Literature as well as criticism – the difference between them being delusive – is condemned (or privileged) to be forever the most rigorous and, consequently, the most unreliable language in terms of which man names and transforms himself.   (de Man 1979, p. 19)

This sentence by the critic Paul de Man is a fair sample of the kind of thinking about literature which is currently termed *deconstruction*. It bristles with the sort of paradox which that thinking finds at work not only in literary texts but in criticism, philosophy and all varieties of discourse, its own included. What can it mean to reject the distinction between literature and criticism as merely a delusion? How can a language be at once the most 'rigorous' and the most 'unreliable' source of knowledge? In what conceivable sense can man 'transform' himself through a process of naming somehow made possible by this rigorous unreliability? These are not problems that either resolve themselves on a more careful reading or simply settle down (like religious belief) into a system of self-supporting paradox. Rather they operate, as more than one disgruntled critic has remarked of de Man, as a positive technique for making trouble; an affront to every normal and comfortable habit of thought.

Deconstruction is a constant reminder of the etymological

link between 'crisis' and 'criticism'. It makes manifest the fact that any radical shift of interpretative thought must always come up against the limits of seeming absurdity. Philosophers have long had to recognize that thinking may lead them inescapably into regions of scepticism such that life could scarcely carry on if people were to act on their conclusions. David Hume (1711–76) called scepticism 'a malady which can never be radically cured, but must return upon us every moment, however we may chase it away. . . . Carelessness and inattention alone can afford us any remedy' (quoted in Russell 1954, p. 697). Deconstruction works at the same giddy limit, suspending all that we take for granted about language, experience and the 'normal' possibilities of human communication. Yet this is not to say that it is a freakish or marginal philosophy, the perverse sport of super-subtle minds disenchanted with the workaday business of literary criticism. Hume saw no way out of his sceptical predicament, except by soothing the mind with careless distractions (billiards was apparently the usual solace of his afternoons). Deconstruction is likewise an activity of thought which cannot be consistently acted on – that way madness lies – but which yet possesses an inescapable rigour of its own.

De Man complains that deconstruction has either been 'dismissed as a harmless academic game' or 'denounced as a terrorist weapon'. Both reactions are understandable, though both – as this book will argue – are equally wide of the mark. Deconstruction is the active antithesis of everything that criticism ought to be if one accepts its traditional values and concepts. Beneath all the age-old conflicts of critical method there has always existed a tacit agreement about certain conventions, or rules of debate, without which (supposedly) no serious thinking about literature could be carried on. That literary texts possessed meaning and that literary criticism sought a knowledge of that meaning – a knowledge with its own proper claims to validity – were principles implicit across the widest divergences of thought. But deconstruction challenges the fundamental distinction between 'literature' and 'criticism' implied by those principles. And it also challenges the idea that criticism provides a special kind of knowledge precisely in so far as its texts don't aspire to 'literary' status. For the deconstructionist, criticism (like philosophy) is always an activity of *writing*, and nowhere more rigorous – to paraphrase de Man – than where it knows and allows for its own 'literary' vagaries.

This is to anticipate whole tracts of argument which will need rehearsing in detail if the reader is to be convinced. Meanwhile I take ambiguous comfort from Derrida's remarks (in *Of Grammatology*) on the strange and deceptive status of 'prefaces' in general. For one thing they are usually – as here! – written last of all and placed up front as a gesture of authorial command. They claim a summarizing function, a power of abstracted systematic statement, which denies the very process and activity of thought involved in the project of writing. Yet they also subvert, in deconstructive fashion, that authority of 'the text' which traditionally attaches to the work itself. As Gayatri Chakravorty Spivak puts it, in her own Translator's Preface to the English version of *Grammatology*:

> the structure preface – text becomes open at both ends. The text has no stable identity, stable origin . . . each act of reading 'the text' is a preface to the next. The reading of a self-professed preface is no exception to this rule.   (Derrida 1977a, p. xii)

In this sense what follows is also a 'preface', a deferred involvement with the writings of Derrida, and not to be taken on trust as a handy and 'objective' survey of deconstructionist method. If there is one applied lesson to be taken away, it is the powerlessness of ready-made concepts to explain or delimit the activity of writing.

I
Roots: structuralism and New Criticism

To present 'deconstruction' as if it were a method, a system or a settled body of ideas would be to falsify its nature and lay oneself open to charges of reductive misunderstanding. Critical theory is nowadays a reputable academic business with a strong vested interest in absorbing and coming to terms with whatever new challenges the times may produce. Structuralism, it is now plain to see, was subject from the outset to a process of adaptation by British and American critics who quickly took heart from what they saw as its 'practical' or 'commonsense' uses. What started as a powerful protest against ruling critical assumptions ended up as just one more available method for saying new things about well-worn texts. By now there is probably a structuralist reading, in one guise or another, of just about every classic of English literature. A few minutes' search through the index of any learned journal is enough to show how structuralism has taken hold in the most respectable and cherished quarters of academic study. Old polemics are quietly forgotten because the ground has meanwhile shifted to such an extent that erstwhile opponents find themselves now in a state of peaceful alliance. To trace this history in detail would provide an instructive example of the capacity of Anglo-American academic criticism to absorb and homogenize any new theory that threatens its sovereign claim.

Deconstruction can be seen in part as a vigilant reaction

against this tendency in structuralist thought to tame and domesticate its own best insights. Some of Jacques Derrida's most powerful essays are devoted to the task of dismantling a concept of 'structure' that serves to immobilize the play of meaning in a text and reduce it to a manageable compass. This process can be seen at work in the reception of a book like Jonathan Culler's *Structuralist Poetics* (1975), regarded (not without reason) as a sound and authoritative guide to the complexities of structuralist thought. Culler's volume has been widely prescribed as student reading by critics and teachers who otherwise show small sympathy with current theoretical developments. Its appeal, one may fairly conjecture, lies partly in its commonsense dealing with problems of interpretative method, and partly in its principled rejection of other, more extreme kinds of theory which would question any such method. Culler makes no secret of his aim to reconcile structuralist theory with a naturalized or intuitive approach to texts. The proper task of theory, in his view, is to provide a legitimating framework or system for insights which a 'competent' reader should be able to arrive at and check against his sense of relevance and fitness. Culler's main claim for the structuralist approach is that it offers a kind of regulative matrix for perceptions that might otherwise seem merely dependent on the critic's personal flair or virtuosity.

His argument becomes strained when it tries to link this notion of readerly 'competence' with an account of the manifold conventions – or arbitrary codes – that make up a literate response. On the one hand Culler appeals to what seems a loose extension of the linguist Noam Chomsky's argument: that linguistic structures are innately programmed in the human mind and operate both as a constraint upon language and as a means of shared understanding. Thus Culler puts the case that our comprehension of literary texts is conditioned by a similar 'grammar' of response which enables us to pick out the relevant structures of meaning from an otherwise inchoate mass of competing detail. On the other hand, he is obliged to recognize that literary texts, unlike the sentences of everyday language, involve certain specialized codes of understanding which have to be acquired and cannot be accounted for in terms of some universal grammar of response. Competence in these terms is a matter of trained intelligence, of justifying one's reading of a text 'by locating it within the conventions of plausibility defined by a generalized knowledge of literature' (Culler 1975, p. 127).

This is structuralism at its most conservative, an outlook that lends support to traditional ideas of the text as a bearer of stable (if complicated) meanings and the critic as a faithful seeker after truth in the text. Culler is evasive about whether these interpretative structures are unchangeably vested in the human mind or whether – as seems more likely – they represent the force of established convention, a kind of second nature to the practised reader. Whatever their status, they clearly imply some manner of check or effective restraint upon the freedoms of critical discourse: hence Culler's doubts (in the final chapter of *Structuralist Poetics*) about the radical claims of those, like Derrida, who seem bent upon dismantling the very bases of interpretative method and meaning.

Deconstruction is avowedly 'post-structuralist' in its refusal to accept the idea of structure as in any sense given or objectively 'there' in a text. Above all, it questions the assumption – so crucial to Culler – that structures of meaning correspond to some deep-laid mental 'set' or pattern of mind which determines the limits of intelligibility. Theory, from Culler's point of view, would be a search for invariant structures or formal universals which reflect the very nature of human intelligence. Literary texts (along with myths, music and other cultural artefacts) yield up their meaning to a mode of analysis possessed of a firm rationale because its sights are set on nothing less than a total explanation of human thought and culture. Theory is assured of its methodological bearings by claiming a deep, universal kinship with the systems of meaning that it proposes to analyse.

Deconstruction, on the contrary, starts out by rigorously *suspending* this assumed correspondence between mind, meaning and the concept of method which claims to unite them.

From Kant to Saussure: the prison-house of concepts

'Kantianism without the transcendental subject' is a description often applied to structuralist thought by those who doubt its validity. Culler's line of argument demonstrates the force of this slogan, showing itself very much akin to the Kantian philosophy of mind and reason. Immanuel Kant (1724–1804) set out to redeem philosophy from the radical scepticism of those, like Hume, who thought it impossible to arrive at any definite, self-validating knowledge of the external world. They had tried and conspicuously failed to discover any necessary link between the laws of thought (or deductive logic) and the nature of real-life events and experience. Thought seemed condemned to a prison-house of reason, endlessly rehearsing its own suppositions but unable to connect them with the world at large. Sensory evidence was no more reliable than ideas like that of cause-and-effect, the 'logic' of which merely reflected or complied with the processes of thought.

Kant saw an escape-route from this condition of deadlocked sceptical reason. It was, he agreed, impossible for consciousness to grasp or 'know' the world in the direct, unmediated form despaired of by Hume and the sceptics. Knowledge was a product of the human mind, the operations of which could only *interpret* the world, and not deliver it up in all its pristine reality. But these very operations, according to Kant, were so deeply vested in human understanding that they offered a new foundation for philosophy. Henceforth philosophy must concern itself not with a delusory quest for 'the real' but with precisely those deep regularities – or *a priori* truths – that constitute human understanding.

It is not hard to see the parallels between Kantian thought and the structuralist outlook presented by a theorist like Culler. Both have their origins in a sceptical divorce between mind and the 'reality' it seeks to understand. In structuralist terms this divorce was most clearly spelled out by the linguist Ferdinand de Saussure. He argued that our knowledge of the world is inextricably shaped and conditioned by the language that serves to represent it. Saussure's insistence on the 'arbitrary' nature of the sign led to his undoing of the natural link that common sense assumes to exist between word and thing. Meanings are bound up, according to Saussure, in a system of relationship and difference that effectively determines our habits of thought and perception. Far from providing a 'window' on reality or (to vary the metaphor) a faithfully reflecting mirror, language brings along with it a whole intricate network of established significations. In his view, our knowledge of things is insensibly structured by the systems of code and convention which alone enable us to classify and organize the chaotic flow of experience. There is simply no access to knowledge except by way of language and other, related orders of representation. Reality is carved up in various ways according to the manifold patterns of sameness and difference which various languages provide. This basic *relativity* of thought and meaning (a theme later taken up by the American linguists Sapir and Whorf) is the starting-point of structuralist theory.

There are, however, various ways of responding to this inaugural insight. Culler exemplifies the Kantian response which strives to keep scepticism at bay by insisting on the normative or somehow self-validating habits of readerly 'competence'. Culler is in search of a generalized theory (or 'poetics') of reading which would fully encompass all the various means we possess for making sense of literary texts. Relativism is thus held in check by an appeal to the reader as a kind of moderating presence, a mind in possession of the requisite intelligence *and* the relevant codes of literate convention. One must, Culler argues, 'have a sense, however undefined, of what one is reading towards' (Culler 1975, p. 163). Interpretation is a quest for order and intelligibility among the manifold possible patterns of sense which the text holds out to a fit reader. The role of a structuralist poetics is partly to explain how these powerful conventions come into play, and partly to draw a line between mere ingenuity and the proper, legitimate or 'competent' varieties of readerly response.

What Culler is proposing in the name of structuralism is a more methodical approach to the kind of criticism that has long been accepted as a staple of academic teaching. The virtue of his theory, from this point of view, is the ease with which it incorporates all manner of examples from other 'pre-structuralist' critics who happen to illustrate the conventions Culler has in mind. There is room within his generalized notion of literary 'competence' for various insights which had often been arrived at without the benefit of any such systematic theory. This follows logically enough from the analogy he draws with Chomskian linguistics. To demonstrate the complex system of rules and transformations underlying a speaker's grammatical utterance is not, of course, to claim any *conscious* knowledge of that system on the speaker's part. Linguistic 'competence', as Chomsky calls it, is tacit and wholly unconscious except when brought to light by the linguist's peculiar and specialized activity. The 'transcendental subject' (or seat of intelligence) in Kantian philosophy is likewise capable of exercising its *a priori* powers without being made in the least aware of them.

Culler adopts the same attitude to critics whose intuitive approach is undeniably fruitful but lacks any larger, organizing theory of valid response. Typical is his treatment of a passage from William Empson's *Seven Types of Ambiguity*, selected for what Culler sees as its all-but-conscious structuralist implications. The 'poem' in question (see Empson 1961, p. 23) is Arthur Waley's translation of a two-line fragment from the Chinese:

> Swiftly the years, beyond recall.
> Solemn the stillness of this spring morning.

Culler remarks how Empson's reading brings out the 'binary oppositions' (mainly the contrast of time-scales) which give the lines their effect. This lends support to Culler's argument that, 'in interpreting a poem, one looks for terms that can be placed on a semantic or thematic axis and opposed to one another' (Culler 1975, p. 126). Such strategies arise from the reader's desire to maximize the interest or significance of a text by discovering its manifold patterns of meaning. A 'competent' reading is one that displays both the acumen required to perceive such meanings and the good sense needed to sort them out from other, less relevant patterns. For his notion of 'relevance' Culler appeals once again to a trans-individual community of judgement assumed to underlie the workings of literate response. Structuralism, with its emphasis on distinctive features and significant contrasts, becomes in effect a *natural extension* or legitimating theory of what it is properly to read a text.

Culler has no real quarrel with those among the 'old' New Critics who talked in terms of irony, paradox or (like Empson) types of ambiguity. These and other patterns of response he regards as enabling conventions, produced by the will to make

sense of texts in a complex and satisfying way. Culler's relatively modest proposal is that critics continue to read in much
the same manner but also reflect on the structures that supposedly govern their various rhetorical notions.

Thus Empson's 'ambiguity' is found to rest on a principle of
binary opposition, the presence of which, in structuralist terms,
does more to explain its suggestive power. Such structures may
not be objectively 'there' in the text but they offer (it is assumed)
so basic and powerful a convention of reading as to place their
validity beyond serious doubt. Culler's poetics, therefore, involves a double *a priori* or regulative claim to knowledge. On the
one hand it presupposes an activity of reading grounded in
certain deeply naturalized codes of understanding. On the
other, it assumes that texts must offer at least sufficient hold – in
the way of contrastive or structural features – for such an
activity to take its own intuitive bearings.

New Critic into structuralist?

Culler's implicit equation between 'structure' and 'competence'
is precisely the kind of interpretative ploy that deconstruction
sets out to challenge. The concept of structure is all too easily
allowed to dominate thought and take on a self-sustaining
objectivity immune to critical reflection. It is on these terms that
structuralism has proved itself a not-too-threatening presence
on the academic scene. Least of all does it now seem a menace –
as traditionalist critics once argued – through its 'scientific'
rigour and taste for abstraction. American New Criticism in its
day attracted the same hostility from those who regarded its
rhetorical bases – 'irony', 'paradox', 'tension' – as so many bits
of monstrous abstract machinery. Yet it soon became clear that,
so far from wanting to rationalize poetry or reduce it to logical
order, the New Critics were bent upon preserving its uniqueness
by fencing it off within the bounds of their chosen rhetoric. The
poem as 'verbal icon', in William K. Wimsatt's phrase, became
the rallying-point of a criticism devoted to the privileged autonomy of poetic language.

If system and structure were prominent in the New Critics'
thinking, the aim was not so much to provide a rationale of
poetic meaning – a logic of logical anomalies – but rather to

build a criticism capable of warding off such rationalist assaults. New Critical method was rational enough in its mode of argumentation but kept a firm distance between its own methodology and the differently organized workings of poetic language. This distance was emphatically preserved by the rules of interpretative conduct which Wimsatt, philosopher-elect of the movement, raised to a high point of principle (see Wimsatt 1954). Chief among these was their attack on the 'heresy of paraphrase', the idea that poetic meaning could be translated into any kind of rational prose equivalent. The poem, in short, was a sacrosanct object whose autonomy demanded a proper respect for the difference between *it* and the language that critics used to describe it.

The New Critics' programme soon took hold as an eminently teachable discipline of literary study. Its erstwhile detractors were easily reconciled to a creed that scarcely challenged the proprieties of critical reason. The same is true of structuralism in its early, scientistic guise. Culler's arguments demonstrate the ease with which a structuralist gloss can be placed upon strategies of reading basically akin to those of the 'old' New Criticism. Academic discourse has little to fear from a 'scientific' criticism – however sweeping its claims – which holds out the promise of a highly self-disciplined knowledge of the text. Such a specialized activity can be allowed to take its place as one among many alternative methods, relied upon to beat its own disciplinary bounds.

Roland Barthes

Culler's poetics of reading is therefore in accord with one powerful strain of structuralist thought. In the early writing of Barthes, among others, the aim was a full-scale science of the text modelled on the linguistics of Saussure and the structural anthropology of Claude Lévi-Strauss. These ambitions were signalled by the widespread structuralist talk of criticism as a 'metalanguage' set up to articulate the codes and conventions of all (existing or possible) literary texts – hence the various efforts to establish a universal 'grammar' of narrative, along with a typology of literary genres based on their predominating figures of language. This view of structuralism as a kind of master-code or analytic discourse upon language is taken by Barthes in his *Elements of Semiology* (1967). Natural language, including the dimension of 'connotative' meaning, is subject to a metalinguistic description which operates in scientific terms and provides a separate or 'second-order' level of understanding. It is evident, according to Barthes, that semiology must be such a meta-language, 'since as a second-order system it takes over a first language (or language-object) which is the system under scrutiny; and this system-object is *signified* through the meta-language of semiology' (Barthes 1967, p. 92). This tortuous explanation really comes down to the belief in structuralist method as a discourse able to master and explain all the varieties of language and culture.

At least this is one way of construing Barthes's text, a reading that brings it into line with accepted ideas of the structuralist activity. There are, however, signs that Barthes was not himself content with so rigid and reductive a programme. If semiology sets up as a second-order discourse unravelling the connotative systems of natural language, why should it then be immune to further operations at a yet higher level of analysis? 'Nothing in principle prevents a meta-language from becoming in its turn the language-object of a new meta-language; this would, for example, be the case with semiology if it were to be "spoken" by another science' (ibid., p. 93).

Barthes is well aware of the dangers and delusions implicit in a discourse that claims the last word in explanatory power. The semiologist may seem to exercise 'the objective function of decipherer' in relation to a world which 'conceals or naturalizes' the meanings of its own dominant culture. But his apparent objectivity is made possible only by a habit of thought which willingly forgets or suppresses its own provisional status. To halt such a process by invoking some ultimate claim to truth is a tactic foreign to the deepest implications of structuralist thought. There is no final analysis, no metalinguistic method, which could possibly draw a rigorous line between its own operations and the language they work upon. Semiology has to recognize that the terms and concepts it employs are always bound up with the signifying process it sets out to analyse. Hence Barthes's insistence that structuralism is always an *activity*, an open-ended practice of reading, rather than a 'method' convinced of its own right reason.

Barthes was alive from the outset to the problems and paradoxes involved in refining structuralist theory without introducing such premature hints of method. To enlist him on the side of deconstruction is perhaps misleading in view of his elusiveness from any theoretical standpoint. Barthes was a brilliant stylist and a highly original – at times even wayward – constructor of theories. His writing was self-conscious to the point where style became an intimate probing of its own possibilities, frequently suggesting theoretical insights but just as often foreclosing them through a sense of resistance to any kind of organized theory. His later texts maintain a dialogue not only with structuralism but with Derrida, Jacques Lacan and other post-structuralist thinkers whose influence Barthes both acknowledges and keeps at a certain protective distance. He remains susceptible as ever to the pleasures of system and method, the old fascination with structure as a totalizing order of thought. But he now seems to view such ideas as 'fantasmatic' images projected by desire upon the polymorphous surface of text, language and culture. The dream of total intelligibility, like 'structure' in its metalinguistic sense, belongs (he implies) to a stage of thinking that is self-blinded by its own conceptual metaphors. The element of rhetorical *play* is present everywhere. Its effects in critical discourse may be ignored, but they are not effaced by the structuralist 'science' of meaning.

This ambivalent attitude to language and structure is one of the themes Barthes takes up in his fragmentary 'autobiography', translated into English in 1977. It might seem an act of supreme 'bad faith' to produce such a work while proclaiming, like Barthes, the 'death of the author' as a wished-for escape from the tyranny of subjectivity. But the reader is soon made aware that Barthes is not to be caught – by anyone except himself – with his textual defences down. He is, as always, shrewdly beforehand with the *hypocrite lecteur* who thinks to ensnare him with simplified versions of his own way of thinking. There is a consummately neat example in Barthes's recollection of an American student ('or positivist, or disputacious: I cannot disentangle') who took it for granted that 'subjectivity' and 'narcissism' were the same thing: 'a matter of speaking well about oneself'. The student was a victim, Barthes reflects,

> of the old couple, the old paradigm: *subjectivity/objectivity*. Yet
> today the subject apprehends himself elsewhere, and subjec-
> tivity can return at another place on the spiral: decon-
> structed, taken apart, shifted, without anchorage: why
> should I not speak of 'myself' since this 'my' is no longer 'the
> self'?   (Barthes 1977, p. 168)

What Barthes in fact offers, by way of autobiography, is a
sequence of deftly turned reflections on the experience of writing, the duplicities of language and the irreducibly *textual* nature
of whatever they communicate. As one such playful alibi (or
'shifter' as Barthes would call it, borrowing the term from
Roman Jakobson), he writes always in the narrative third
person, addressing the various topics of his own obsessive
interest with a kind of quizzical detachment. As the book's
epigraph helpfully suggests, 'it should all be considered as if
spoken by a character in a novel'.

Barthes undermines not only the natural conventions of
language but also those methods (his own included) that claim
to have mastered their working. The early, 'structuralist'
Barthes is called to account by this later *alter ego* for his pursuit of
system and method, a deluded quest but still a source of
considerable pleasure. The dialogue-of-one becomes a kind of
mocking catechism:

> You keep the notion of 'meta-language', but in the category of
> image-reservoir. This is a constant procedure in your work:
> you use a pseudo-linguistics, a metaphorical linguistics . . .
> these concepts come to constitute allegories, a second lan-
> guage, whose abstraction is diverted to fictive ends. . . . And
> meaning itself – when you watch it functioning, you do so
> with the almost puerile amusement of a buyer who never tires
> of pulling the switch of some gadget.   (ibid., p. 124)

This perfectly catches the movement of thought by which
Barthes manages to 'discompose' his own ideas and restore
them to a textual dimension evoking all the suppleness and
vagaries of pure linguistic play.

This aspect of Barthes marks the point at which deconstruction begins to shake and unsettle the structuralist project. It has

been quietly passed over by critics anxious to domesticate structuralism by presenting it as a 'method' sometimes outlandish in its claims but basically amenable to commonsense uses. The apparent eccentricities of Barthes's later writing are mostly regarded as harmless whimsical diversions on the part of a critic who required some form of 'creative' escape from the exigencies of high-powered theory. This attitude, typical of Anglo-American criticism, draws a firm line between the discipline of *thinking* about texts and the activity of writing which that discipline is supposed to renounce or ignore in its own performance. Criticism as 'answerable style' (in Geoffrey Hartman's phrase) is an idea that cuts right across the deep-grained assumptions of academic discourse. It is, as I shall argue, one of the most unsettling and radical departures of deconstructionist thought. A properly attentive reading of Barthes brings out the extent to which critical concepts are ceaselessly transformed or undone by the activity of self-conscious writing.

This vertiginous textual movement is resisted by readers who see no connection between the 'structuralist' Barthes and the wayward, dandified discourse of his later writings. Such a reader is Philip Thody, whose book on Barthes (subtitled *A Conservative Estimate*) presents him as a gifted but erratic thinker, full of good ideas but apt to go off at an embarrassing tangent (Thody 1977). Thody is convinced that beneath all the fireworks there is a structure of assumptions not so very different from those of the old New Criticism. Barthes is on the one hand a dazzling performer, a master of verbal subterfuge, and, on the other, a decently methodical thinker dressed up in the current Parisian style. His subversive tactics come down to an inordinate fondness for paradox disguising a commitment to order and method.

Thody's recuperative reading is plainly intended to make sense of Barthes for conservative-minded British consumers. His bluff commonsensical tone combines with the attitude that neatly drives a wedge between the acceptable face of structuralist *method* and its other, more radical implications. Hence his slight impatience with Barthes's paradoxical strain, a tendency Thody regards as peripheral and probably betraying some strong but repressed 'creative' drive. That paradox might be at the root of Barthes's thinking, rather than merely an ornament of 'style', is a notion scarcely to be entertained. Yet this is precisely the import of numerous passages in his writing which show Barthes consciously confronting reason and method with twists of argument beyond their power of absorption. One of the fragments from his pseudo-autobiography makes this 'reactive formation' the source and motive of all Barthes's writing.

> A *doxa* (a popular opinion) is formulated, intolerable; to free myself of it, I postulate a paradox; then this paradox turns bad, becomes a new concretion, itself becomes a new *doxa*, and I must seek further for a new paradox. (Barthes 1977, p. 71)

Thody's attitude reflects a belief that paradox and suchlike figures of thought belong to the province of 'literary' language and can play only a marginal or self-indulgent role in criticism. It is the same demarcation that the New Critics set between the figural devices of poetry and the rational language of prose explication.

This boundary was always subject to periodic raids and incursions by the more adventurous New Critics, especially those poets and novelists among them who felt uneasy with a discipline that placed one aspect of their writing at such a remove from the other. The issue was more than a matter of critical technique. What the orthodox New Critics sought in the language of poetry was a structure somehow transcending human reason and ultimately pointing to a religious sense of values. Walter Ong makes the point most effectively in his essay 'Wit and Mystery'. There is a direct relation, he argues, between the New Critics' emphasis on poetic 'wit' (with its correlative figures of irony, paradox, etc.) and their general allegiance to Christian belief: 'At the point to which the trail of wit leads, the very texture of poetry itself . . . is seen to come into fundamental contact with the heart of Christian doctrine' (Ong 1962, p. 90). R. P. Blackmur reaches a similar conclusion in discussing the role of poetic 'analogy', the way in which poems can suggest without stating the conflicts and tensions of existence: 'Only in analogy are the opposites identical . . . and it was a similar perception which led Saint Augustine to say that in every poem there is some of the substance of God' (Blackmur 1967, pp. 42–3). It thus becomes a matter of deep doctrinal commitment that criticism should respect the peculiar sanctions of poetic language and restrict its own operations to the separate realm of rational prose statement. To confuse the two is to break down the disciplined awareness which strives to preserve the authentic 'mystery' of poetic truth.

Thus the autonomy of poetry became not merely an issue in aesthetics but a testing-point of faith in relation to human reason. Behind the New Critical rhetoric of irony and paradox is a whole metaphysics of language, where poetic and religious claims to truth are bound up together. At the same time there were those who assented in principle to this discipline of thought but found it in practice hard, if not impossible, to live with. Allen Tate, for instance, adhered to the basic New Critical belief that poetic 'tension' and 'paradox' were the hallmarks of a knowledge superior to reason and linked to the ineffable certitudes of faith. Yet he also wrote of the 'intolerable' strain imposed upon the critical mind by the very nature of its 'middle position between imagination and philosophy' (Tate 1953, p. 111). Tate, like Blackmur in his speculative moments, seems to be struggling with the protocols of New Critical belief and venturing – albeit very warily – on to different ground. Take the following passage from Blackmur's *A Primer of Ignorance*:

> Just as the imagination is never able to get all of itself into the arbitrary forms of art and has to depend on aids from the intellect, from conventions . . . so the intellect in dealing with imagination is itself imperfect and has to depend upon conventions of its own, some quite formalistic. (Blackmur 1967, pp. 77–8)

Blackmur and Tate are both uneasily aware that the languages of literature and criticism by no means obey the rigid territorial imperative laid down by orthodox fiat.

Beyond New Criticism

The challenge became stronger when critics like Geoffrey Hartman announced their intention of breaking altogether with New Critical method and moving 'beyond formalism'. That the stakes were more than aesthetically loaded is clear from the response of rearguard New Critics, including W. K. Wimsatt, whose essay 'Battering the Object' (1970) sought to recall American criticism to its proper methods and ends. Wimsatt was defensively reacting to a new school of thought which questioned the privileged autonomy of poetic form and claimed a much greater degree of speculative freedom for the literary critic. The sources of this thought were in continental theory, and its American representatives – among them Paul de Man and J. Hillis Miller – were later to become the protagonists of deconstruction.

It is possible, then, to make out a parallel shift of awareness affecting both the structuralist activity and the deep-laid foundations of American New Criticism. It would, of course, be wrong to push this parallel too far. Structuralist theory never took on the kind of quasi-religious orthodoxy invoked by New Critical method. But it was, as I have tried to show, subject to various domesticating pressures which effectively sealed off its more disturbing implications. Culler's appeal to the moderating judgement of the 'competent' reader is one such response, attempting to ground critical theory in an all-but-transcendental philosophy of mind. Thody's treatment of Barthes is a cruder but no less determined effort to isolate what is useful and methodical and consign the rest to a harmless realm of stylistic indulgence. New Criticism and structuralism each had its orthodox side, an aspect that lent itself to wholly conformable uses. At the same time they both tended to generate, in livelier minds, a sense of unease or frustration which called their very methods into question.

For American critics the waning of New Critical hegemony coincided with a sudden new interest in French theoretical ideas. This came at a time when structuralism was already being subjected (in the texts of Derrida especially) to a searching critique of its own suppositions and methodical claims. The effect of this convergence is manifest in the writings of Geoffrey Hartman, J. Hillis Miller and others whose passage 'beyond formalism' led them, through various stages, to what is now a deconstructionist position. In 1970 Hartman was still finding it difficult to imagine where this speculative quest might lead to. 'To go beyond formalism', he wrote (1970, p. 113), 'is as yet too hard for us and may even be, unless we are Hegelians believing in absolute spirit, against the nature of understanding.' His state of perplexity recalls the problems faced by Blackmur and Tate in their speculative musings. The difference lies partly in Hartman's rejection of any absolute doctrinal adherence, and partly in the much wider range of ideas created by structuralist debate.

These new-found freedoms are very much at work in Hartman's essay on Milton, which exuberantly breaks with New Critical assumptions about language, style and the place of critical theory (see 'Adam on the Grass with Balsamum', in Hartman 1970). That Milton should be chosen as fighting ground is further indication of the challenge being offered to New Critical opinion. The New Critics mostly followed Eliot in using the 'problem' of Milton's style as a cover for their deep dislike of his radicalism in politics and religion. Hartman sets out to overturn this powerful consensus. He defends not only Milton's style but the critic's freedom to adopt a charged and 'answerable' style of his own in order to counter the weight of received opinion. Hartman wants to initiate 'a more adventurous hermeneutic tradition, even at the risk of deepening, provisionally, the difference between criticism and interpretation'. By 'criticism' Hartman means that disciplined and self-denying ordinance of method which keeps a safe distance between the literary text and the discourse that seeks to comprehend it. The 'hermeneutic' tradition, on the other hand, takes account of the interpreter's puzzles and perplexities by *including* them within the terms of a full and generous response. Such a style is 'answerable' in its sense of the constant provisional adjustments the critic has to make between theory and text. It thus works to forestall any cramping or excessively rigid method.

Hartman, like Barthes, asserts the critic's freedom to exploit a style that actively transforms and questions the nature of interpretative thought. In itself this marks a decisive break with the scrupulous decorum of critical language maintained in Eliot's wake. Eliot famously defined the 'perfect critic' as one who showed 'intelligence itself swiftly operating the analysis of sensation to the point of principle and definition'. This is to argue that theory, in so far as it is valid at all, is strictly a matter of placing some orderly construction upon the 'immediate' data of perception. Barthes and Hartman totally reject this careful policing of the bounds between literature and theory. Where

Eliot proposes a disciplined or educating movement of thought from perception to principle, they discover an endlessly fascinating conflict, the 'scene' of which is the text itself in its alternating aspects of knowledge and pleasurable fantasy.

This is deconstruction in one of its modes: a deliberate attempt to turn the resources of interpretative style against any too rigid convention of method or language. It emerged, as we have seen, through the impingement of post-structuralist thought on an American New Critical tradition already showing symptoms of internal strain and self-doubt. But deconstruction has another, more toughly argumentative aspect which starts out from similar questioning motives but pursues them to a different end. Its readings, though suspicious of method and system, are themselves rigorously argued and as remote from Hartman's virtuoso language as Hartman is from the academic style he seeks to explode. Jacques Derrida is the philosophic source of this powerful critique, and Paul de Man at present its foremost American exponent.

In the hands of less subtle and resourceful readers deconstruction can become – it is all too clear – a theoretical vogue as uniform and cramping as the worst New Critical dogma. At best it has provided the impetus for a total revaluation of interpretative theory and practice, the effects of which have yet to be fully absorbed.

2
Jacques Derrida:
language against itself

The texts of Jacques Derrida defy classification according to any of the clear-cut boundaries that define modern academic discourse. They belong to 'philosophy' in so far as they raise certain familiar questions about thought, language, identity and other longstanding themes of philosophical debate. Moreover, they raise those questions through a form of critical dialogue with previous texts, many of which (from Plato to Husserl and Heidegger) are normally assigned to the history of philosophic thought. Derrida's professional training was as a student of philosophy (at the École Normale Supérieure in Paris, where he now teaches), and his writings demand of the reader a considerable knowledge of the subject. Yet Derrida's texts are like nothing else in modern philosophy, and indeed represent a challenge to the whole tradition and self-understanding of that discipline.

One way of describing this challenge is to say that Derrida refuses to grant philosophy the kind of privileged status it has always claimed as the sovereign dispenser of reason. Derrida confronts this claim to power on its own chosen ground. He argues that philosophers have been able to impose their various systems of thought only by ignoring, or suppressing, the disruptive effects of language. His aim is always to draw out these effects by a critical reading which fastens on, and skilfully unpicks, the elements of metaphor and other figurative devices at work in the texts of philosophy. Deconstruction in this, its most rigorous form acts as a constant reminder of the ways in which language deflects or complicates the philosopher's project. Above all, deconstruction works to undo the idea – according to Derrida, the ruling illusion of Western metaphysics – that reason can somehow dispense with language and arrive at a pure, self-authenticating truth or method. Though philosophy strives to efface its textual or 'written' character, the signs of that struggle are there to be read in its blind-spots of metaphor and other rhetorical strategies.

In this sense Derrida's writings seem more akin to literary criticism than philosophy. They rest on the assumption that modes of rhetorical analysis, hitherto applied mainly to literary texts, are in fact indispensable for reading *any* kind of discourse, philosophy included. Literature is no longer seen as a kind of poor relation to philosophy contenting itself with mere 'imaginary' themes and forgoing any claim to philosophic dignity and truth. This attitude has, of course, a long prehistory in Western tradition. It was Plato who expelled the poets from his ideal republic, who set up reason as a guard against the false beguilements of rhetoric, and who called forth a series of critical 'defences' and 'apologies' which runs right through from Sir Philip Sidney to I. A. Richards and the American New Critics. The lines of defence have been variously drawn up, according to whether the critic sees himself as *contesting* philosophy on its own argumentative ground, or as operating outside its reach on a different – though equally privileged – ground.

In the latter camp it is F. R. Leavis who has most forcefully asserted the critic's right to dissociate his habits of thought from the logical checks and procedures demanded of philosophic discourse. Criticism on Leavis's terms is a matter of communicating deep-laid intuitive responses, which analysis can point to and persuasively *enact*, but which it can by no means *explain* or *theorize* about. Philosophy is kept at arm's length by treating literary language as a medium of 'lived' or 'felt' experience, a region where the critic's 'mature' responses are his only reliable guide and where there is no support to be had from abstract methodology. Hence Leavis's insistence on the virtues of 'practical' criticism (or close reading), allied to such moral imperatives as 'relevance', 'maturity' and an 'open reverence before life'. The effect of this programme is to draw a firm line of demarcation between literary language and the problems of philosophy. Leavis rejects the idea that criticism need concern itself with epistemological problems, or rhetorical modes of working, implicit in literary texts. His ideal critic works within a discipline defined by qualities of responsiveness and intuitive tact, rather than subtlety of philosophic grasp.

Such was the tenor of Leavis's famous 'reply' to Rene Wellek, who had asked (in an otherwise appreciative essay) why Leavis should not provide a more coherent or worked-out rationale for his critical judgements (see Leavis 1937). To do so would amount to a betrayal, it seemed, of the different but equally disciplined activity required of the literary critic. That activity was justified in so far as it preserved the life-giving wholeness of critical response from the deadening weight of abstract theory.

Leavis represents the most rooted and uncompromising form of resistance to philosophy on the part of literary criticism. The American New Critics, with their penchant for rhetorical system and method, tended to strike a somewhat more ambiguous stance. I have already quoted Allen Tate, in speculative mood, writing despairingly of criticism as a middle-ground activity torn between the warring poles of imagination and philosophic reason. Typically, the New Critics managed to contain these tensions by devising a rhetoric of figure and paradox which closed the poem off within its own formal limits. Poetry (and fiction, so far as they dealt with it) took on a kind of self-authenticating status, confirmed by the various dogmas of critical method. Conceptual problems – like that of relating poetic 'form' to communicable 'meaning' – were neatly side-stepped by being treated as if they were somehow constitutive of poetry's uniquely complex mode of existence. Paradox and irony, which Tate saw as bearing (to some extent at least) on the critic's own predicament, were generally regarded by the New Criticism as objectively 'there' in the poem's structure of meaning.

Hence the circularity and self-sufficient character of New Critical rhetoric. It kept philosophy at bay, not, like Leavis, by flatly denying its relevance, but by translating its questions into a language of irreducibly *aesthetic* paradox and tension. As critics came to interrogate this rhetoric of closure, so it became more evident that the problems had merely been repressed or displaced, and that criticism had yet to discover its relation to the modes and exigencies of 'philosophic' discourse. It was at this point in the history of American criticism and its discontents that Derrida's influence came as such a liberating force. His work provided a whole new set of powerful strategies which placed the literary critic, not simply on a footing with the philosopher, but in a complex relationship (or rivalry) with him, whereby philosophic claims were open to rhetorical questioning or *deconstruction*. Paul de Man has described this process of thought in which 'literature turns out to be the main topic of philosophy and the model of the kind of truth to which it aspires' (de Man 1979, p. 113). Once alerted to the *rhetorical* nature of philosophic arguments, the critic is in a strong position to reverse the age-old prejudice against literature as a debased or merely deceptive form of language. It now becomes possible to argue – indeed, impossible to deny – that literary texts are less deluded than the discourse of philosophy, precisely because they implicitly acknowledge and exploit their own rhetorical status. Philosophy comes to seem, in de Man's work, 'an endless reflection on its own destruction at the hands of literature'.

Derrida's attentions are therefore divided between 'literary' and 'philosophical' texts, a distinction which in practice he constantly breaks down and shows to be based on a deep but untenable prejudice. His readings of Mallarmé, Valéry, Genet and Sollers are every bit as rigorous as his essays on philosophers like Hegel and Husserl. Literary texts are not fenced off inside some specialized realm of figurative licence where rational commentary fears to tread. Unlike the New Critics, Derrida has no desire to establish a rigid demarcation of zones between literary language and critical discourse. On the contrary, he sets out to show that certain kinds of paradox are produced across all the varieties of discourse by a motivating impulse which runs so deep in Western thought that it respects none of the conventional boundaries. Criticism, philosophy, linguistics, anthropology, the whole modern gamut of 'human sciences' – all are at some point subjected to Derrida's relentless critique. This is the most important point to grasp about deconstruction. There is no language so vigilant or self-aware that it can effectively escape the conditions placed upon thought by its own prehistory and ruling metaphysic.

Blindness and Insight: deconstructing the New Criticism

The passage 'beyond formalism' was broached in various ways. Some critics (like Geoffrey Hartman) have adopted a wayward and teasingly indirect style, while others – notably Paul de Man – have attempted to *think through* the paradoxes of New Critical method. De Man's essays in *Blindness and Insight* (1971) were a powerful application of Derridean ideas to the rhetoric of modern poetics. To read the New Critics with an eye to their founding metaphors is to discover, in de Man's terminology, a 'blindness' inseparable from their moments of greatest 'insight'. Their formalist notion of the poem as 'verbal icon' – a timeless, self-possessed structure of meaning – is shown to deconstruct its own claim through unrecognized twists of implication. Their obsession with 'organic' form was undermined by those very 'ambiguities' and 'tensions' which they sought out in order to praise, and so contain, them. 'This unitarian criticism', as de Man puts it, 'finally becomes a criticism of ambiguity, an ironic reflection on the absence of the unity it had postulated' (de Man 1971, p. 28). 'Form' itself turns out to be more an operative fiction, a product of the interpreter's rage for order, than anything vested in the literary work itself. The organicist metaphors of New Critical parlance result from what de Man calls the 'dialectical interplay' set up between text and interpreter. 'Because such patient and delicate attention was paid to the reading of forms, the critic pragmatically entered into the hermeneutic circle of interpretation, mistaking it for the organic circularity of natural processes' (ibid., p. 29).

Deconstruction draws no line between the kind of close reading appropriate to a 'literary' text and the strategies required to draw out the subtler implications of critical language. Since *all* forms of writing run up against perplexities of meaning and intent, there is no longer any question of a privileged status for literature and a secondary, self-effacing role for the language of criticism. De Man fully accepts the Derridean principle that 'writing', with its own dialectic of blindness and insight, pre-cedes all the categories that conventional wisdom has tried to impose on it.

This amounts to a downright refusal of the system of prior-ities which has traditionally governed the relation between 'criti-cal' and 'creative' language. That distinction rested on the idea that literary texts embodied an authentic or self-possessed plenitude of meaning which criticism could only hint at by its roundabout strategies of reading. For Derrida, this is yet another sign of the rooted Western prejudice which tries to reduce writing – or the 'free play' of language – to a stable meaning equated with the character of *speech*. In spoken lan-guage (so the implication runs), meaning is 'present' to the speaker through an act of inward self-surveillance which en-sures a perfect, intuitive 'fit' between intention and utterance. Literary texts have been accorded the status of a self-authenticated meaning and truth, a privilege deriving (in Der-rida's view) from the deep mistrust of textuality which pervades Western attitudes to language. This mystique of origins and presence can best be challenged by annulling the imaginary boundaries of discourse, the various territorial imperatives which mark off 'literature' from 'criticism', or 'philosophy' from everything that stands outside its traditional domain.

This redistribution of discourse implies some very drastic shifts in our habits of reading. For one thing, it means that critical texts must be read in a radically different way, not so much for their interpretative 'insights' as for the symptoms of 'blindness' which mark their conceptual limits. De Man puts the case most succinctly:

> Since they are not scientific, critical texts have to be read with the same awareness of ambivalence that is brought to the study of non-critical literary texts, and since the rhetoric of their discourse depends on categorical statements, the dis-crepancy between meaning and assertion is a constitutive part of their logic.   (ibid., p. 110)

This argument cuts both ways when it comes to defining the critic's position *vis-à-vis* the literary text. Clearly it denies him the kind of methodical or disciplined approach which has been the recurrent dream of a certain critical tradition. On the other hand it offers a way beyond the rigid separation of roles which would cast him as a mere attendant upon the sovereign word of the text. What it loses in methodical self-assurance, criticism stands to regain in rhetorical interest on its own account. A similar reversal of priorities occurs in the deconstructive reading of 'literary' texts. There is no longer the sense of a primal authority attaching to the literary work and requiring that criticism keep its respectful distance. The autonomy of the text is actively invaded by a new and insubordinate style of commentary which puts in question all the traditional attributes of literary meaning. But at the same time this questioning raises literature to a point of rhetorical complexity and interest where its moments of 'blindness' are often more acutely revealing than anything in the discourse of philosophy.

Such has been the effect of Derrida's writing on a deeply entrenched conservative tradition – that of American New Criticism – which had already started to question its own ideology. What might have carried on as a series of skirmishing tactics (or virtuoso exercises in Hartman's manner) was galvanized by Derrida into something far more radical and deeply unsettling. We can now look more closely at the major texts in which Derrida sets forth the terms and implications of deconstructive reading. Rather than take his books one by one, I shall fasten upon certain crucial themes and argumentative strategies, acting as far as possible on Derrida's reiterated warning that his texts are not a store of ready-made 'concepts' but an *activity* resistant to any such reductive ploy.

Language, writing, *differance*

If there is a single theme which draws together the otherwise disparate field of 'structuralist' thought, it is the principle – first enounced by Saussure – that language is a *differential* network of meaning. There is no self-evident or one-to-one link between 'signifier' and 'signified', the word as (spoken or written) vehicle and the concept it serves to evoke. Both are caught up in a play of distinctive features where differences of sound and sense are the only markers of meaning. Thus, at the simplest phonetic level, *bat* and *cat* are distinguished (and meaning is generated) by the switching of initial consonants. The same is true of *bag* and *big*, with their inter-substitution of vowels. Language is in this sense *diacritical*, or dependent on a structured economy of differences which allows a relatively small range of linguistic elements to signify a vast repertoire of negotiable meanings.

Saussure went on from this cardinal insight to construct what has become a dominant working programme for modern linguistics. His proposals broke with traditional thinking in two main respects. He argued, first, that linguistics could be placed on a scientific basis only by adopting a 'synchronic' approach, one that treated language as a network of structural relations existing at a given point in time. Such a discipline would have to renounce – or provisionally suspend – the 'diachronic' methods of historical research and speculation which had dominated nineteenth-century linguistics. Second, Saussure found it necessary to make a firm distinction between the isolated speech-act or utterance (*parole*) and the general system of articulate relationships from which it derived (*la langue*). This system, he reasoned, had to underlie and pre-exist any possible sequence of speech, since meaning could be produced only in accordance with the organizing ground-rules of language.

Structuralism, in all its manifold forms and applications, developed in the wake of Saussure's founding programme for modern linguistics. This is not the place for a detailed account of that development, which the reader will find expounded in Terence Hawkes's *Structuralism and Semiotics* (1977). Briefly, structuralism took over from Saussure the idea that *all* cultural systems – not only language – could be studied from a 'synchronic' viewpoint which would bring out their various related levels of signifying activity.

The precise status of linguistics in regard to this new-found enterprise was a topic of considerable debate. Saussure had argued that language was but one of many codes, and that linguistics should therefore not expect to retain its methodological pre-eminence. With the advent of a fully fledged *semiotics*, or science of signs, language would assume its proper,

participant place in the social life of signs in general. Paradoxically, it was Roland Barthes – the most versatile of structuralist
thinkers – who originally wanted to reverse this perspective and
reinstate linguistics as the master-science of semiology. Barthes
was quick to exploit the possibilities of structuralist method
across a diverse field of cultural codes, from literary texts to
cookery, fashion and photography. Yet in his *Elements of Semiology* (1967) Barthes is to be found expressing the conviction
that 'the moment we go on to systems where the sociological
significance is more than superficial, we are once more confronted with language'. And this, he explains, because 'we are,
much more than in former times . . . a civilization of the
written word' (Barthes 1967, p. 10).

Of course, this text belongs to an early stage of Barthes's
development, a phase he was later to criticize precisely for its
overdependence on concepts of metalinguistic or 'scientific'
knowledge. I showed in Chapter 1 how far he eventually
travelled toward deconstructing such concepts through a textual activity aware of its own shifting and provisional status.
But the kind of linguistic analogy that Barthes once deployed is
representative of structuralism at a certain definite point in its
development. It was at this point that Derrida intervened, with
the object of wrenching structuralism away from what he saw as
its residual attachment to a Western metaphysics of meaning
and presence. In particular, he questioned the role of linguistics
in   dictating   the   methodological   priorities   of   structuralist
thought. Derrida's critique of Saussure, in his essay 'Linguistics
and Grammatology' (in Derrida 1977a, pp. 27–73), is therefore
a crucial point of encounter for the deconstructive enterprise.

The argument turns on Saussure's attitude to the relative
priority of *spoken* as opposed to *written* language, a dualism
Derrida locates at the heart of Western philosophic tradition.
He cites a number of passages from Saussure in which writing is
treated as a merely derivative or secondary form of linguistic
notation, always dependent on the primary reality of speech
and the sense of a speaker's 'presence' behind his words.
Derrida finds a dislocating tension here, a problem that other
structuralists (Barthes included) had been content to regard as
a puzzling but unavoidable paradox. What are we to make of
this privileged status for speech (*parole*) in a theory which is

otherwise so heavily committed to the prior significance of language-as-system (*langue*)? Barthes presents the question most succinctly:

A language does not exist properly except in 'the speaking mass'; one cannot handle speech except by drawing on the language. But conversely, a language is possible only starting from speech; historically, speech phenomena always precede language phenomena (it is speech which makes language evolve), and genetically, a language is constituted in the individual through his learning from the environmental speech. (Barthes 1967, p. 16)

The relation of language and speech is thus 'dialectical'; it sets in train a process of thought which shuttles productively from one standpoint to the other.

Where Derrida differs with Barthes is in his refusal simply to accept this paradox as part of a larger, encompassing project (that of semiology) which would overcome such apparent contradictions. For Derrida, there is a fundamental *blindness* involved in the Saussurian text, a failure to think through the problems engendered by its own mode of discourse. What is repressed there, along with 'writing' in its common or restricted sense, is the idea of language as a signifying system which exceeds all the bounds of individual 'presence' and speech. Looking back over the passage from Barthes quoted above, one can see how 'speech' terminology prevails, even where the argument is ostensibly stating the rival claims of language-as-system. Thus Barthes (drawing on Saussure) refers metaphorically to 'the speaking mass' in a context which purportedly invokes the totality of language, but which appeals even so to actual speakers and their speech as the source of that totality. Barthes may state, as a matter of principle, that language is at once the 'product and the instrument' of speech, that their relationship is always 'dialectical' and not to be reduced to any clear-cut priority. In practice, however, his theorizing leans upon metaphors which implicitly privilege individual speech above the system of meaning that sustains it.

Derrida's line of attack is to pick out such loaded metaphors and show how they work to support a whole powerful structure of presuppositions. If Saussure was impelled, like others before him, to relegate writing to a suspect or secondary status, then the mechanisms of that repression are there in his text and open to a deconstructive reading. Thus Derrida sets out to demonstrate

1 that writing is systematically degraded in Saussurian linguistics;
2 that this strategy runs up against suppressed but visible contradictions;
3 that by following these contradictions through one is led *beyond* linguistics to a 'grammatology', or science of writing and textuality in general.

Derrida sees a whole metaphysics at work behind the privilege granted to speech in Saussure's methodology. *Voice* becomes a metaphor of truth and authenticity, a source of self-present 'living' speech as opposed to the secondary lifeless emanations of writing. In speaking one is able to experience (supposedly) an intimate link between sound and sense, an inward and immediate realization of meaning which yields itself up without reserve to perfect, transparent understanding. Writing, on the contrary, destroys this ideal of pure self-presence. It obtrudes an alien, depersonalized medium, a deceiving shadow which falls between intent and meaning, between utterance and understanding. It occupies a promiscuous public realm where authority is sacrificed to the vagaries and whims of textual 'dissemination'. Writing, in short, is a threat to the deeply traditional view that associates truth with self-presence and the 'natural' language wherein it finds expression.

Against this tradition Derrida argues what at first must seem an extraordinary case: that writing is in fact the *precondition* of language and must be conceived as prior to speech. This involves showing, to begin with, that the concept of writing cannot be reduced to its normal (i.e. graphic or inscriptional) sense. As Derrida deploys it, the term is closely related to that element of signifying *difference* which Saussure thought essential to the workings of language. Writing, for Derrida, is the 'free play' or element of undecidability within every system of communication. Its operations are precisely those which escape the self-consciousness of speech and its deluded sense of the mastery of concept over language. Writing is the endless displacement of meaning which both governs language and places it for ever beyond the reach of a stable, self-authenticating knowledge. In this sense, oral language already belongs to a 'generalized writing', the effects of which are everywhere disguised by the illusory 'metaphysics of presence'. Language is always inscribed in a network of relays and differential 'traces' which can never be grasped by the individual speaker. What Saussure calls the 'natural bond' between sound and sense – the guaranteed self-knowledge of speech – is in fact a delusion engendered by the age-old repression of a 'feared and subversive' writing. To question that bond is to venture into regions as yet uncharted, and requires a rigorous effort of conceptual desublimation or 'waking up'. Writing is that which exceeds – and has the power to dismantle – the whole traditional edifice of Western attitudes to thought and language.

The repression of writing lies deep in Saussure's proposed methodology. It shows in his refusal to consider any form of linguistic notation outside the phonetic-alphabetical script of Western culture. As opposed, that is, to the non-phonetic varieties which Derrida often discusses: hieroglyphs, algebraic notions, formalized languages of different kinds. This 'phonocentric' bias is closely allied, in Derrida's view, to the underlying structure of assumptions which links Saussure's project to Western metaphysics. So long as writing is treated as a more or less faithful transcription of the elements of speech, its effects can be safely contained within that massive tradition. As Derrida puts it:

> The system of language associated with phonetic-alphabetic writing is that within which logocentric metaphysics, determining the sense of being as presence, has been produced. This logocentrism, this *epoch* of the full speech, has always placed in parenthesis, *suspended*, and suppressed for essential reasons, all free reflection on the origin and status of writing.   (Derrida 1977a, p. 43)

There is a deep connection between the craving for self-presence, as it affects the philosophy of language, and the 'phonocentrism' which prevents linguistic method from effectively broaching the question of writing. Both are components of a powerful metaphysic which works to confirm the 'natural' priority of speech.

Derrida shows that these assumptions, though consistent and mutually reinforcing at a certain level, lie open to disruption as soon as one substitutes 'writing' for 'speech' in the conceptual order that governs them. The effect is unsettling not only for linguistics but for every field of enquiry based on the idea of an immediate, intuitive access to meaning. Derrida traces the exclusion or degradation of writing as a gesture perpetually re-enacted in the texts of Western philosophy. It occurs wherever reason looks for a ground or authenticating method immune to the snares of textuality. If meaning could only attain to a state of self-sufficient intelligibility, language would no longer present any problem but serve as an obedient vehicle of thought. To pose the question of writing in its radical, Derridean form is thus to transgress – or 'violently' oppose – the conventional relation of language and thought.

Such is the deconstructive violence to which Derrida subjects the texts of Saussure and his structuralist successors. It is not a question, he repeats, of rejecting the entire Saussurian project or denying its historical significance. Rather it is a matter of driving that project to its ultimate conclusions and seeing where those conclusions work to challenge the project's conventional premises. In Derrida's words,

> It is when he is not expressly dealing with writing, when he feels he has closed the parentheses on that subject, that Saussure opens the field of a general grammatology . . . then one realizes that what was chased off limits, the wandering outcast of linguistics, has indeed never ceased to haunt language as its primary and most intimate possibility. Then something which was never spoken and which is nothing other than writing itself as the origin of language writes itself in Saussure's discourse.   (ibid., pp. 43–4)

Saussure is thus not merely held up as one more exemplar of a blind and self-deceiving tradition. Derrida makes it clear that structuralism, whatever its conceptual limits, was a necessary stage on the way to deconstruction. Saussure set the terms for a development which passed beyond the grasp of his explicit programme but which could hardly have been formulated otherwise. By repressing the problem which his own theory of language all but brought into view, Saussure transcended the express limitations of that theory. The very concept of 'writing' was enlarged through this encounter into something primordial and far removed from its place in traditional usage.

The point will bear repeating: deconstruction is not simply a strategic reversal of categories which otherwise remain distinct and unaffected. It seeks to undo both a given order of priorities *and* the very system of conceptual opposition that makes that order possible. Thus Derrida is emphatically *not* trying to prove that 'writing' in its normal, restricted sense is somehow more basic than speech. On the contrary, he agrees with Saussure that linguistics had better not yield uncritically to the 'prestige' that written texts have traditionally enjoyed in Western culture. If the opposition speech/writing is not subjected to a full critique, it remains 'a blind prejudice', one which (in Derrida's phrase) 'is no doubt common to the accused and the prosecutor'. Deconstruction is better provided with texts, like Saussure's, which foreground the problematic status of writing precisely by adopting a traditional perspective. A repressed writing then reasserts itself most forcibly through the detours and twists of implication discovered in Saussure. It is the 'tension between gesture and statement' in such critical texts which 'liberates the future of a general grammatology'.

Deconstruction is therefore an activity of reading which remains closely tied to the texts it interrogates, and which can never set up independently as a self-enclosed system of operative concepts. Derrida maintains an extreme and exemplary scepticism when it comes to defining his own methodology. The deconstructive leverage supplied by a term like *writing* depends on its resistance to any kind of settled or definitive meaning. To call it a 'concept' is to fall straight away into the trap of imagining some worked-out scheme of hierarchical ideas in which 'writing' would occupy its own, privileged place. We have seen (in Chapter 1) how structuralism proved itself amenable to such uses. The *concept* of structure is easily kidnapped by a tame methodology which treats it as a handy organizing theme and ignores its unsettling implications. Derrida perceives the same process at work in the structured economy of differential features which Saussure described as the precondition of language. Once the term is fixed within a given explanatory system, it becomes (like 'structure') usable in ways that deny or suppress its radical insights.

Hence Derrida's tactical recourse to a shifting battery of terms which cannot be reduced to any single, self-identical meaning. *Differance* is perhaps the most effective of these, since it sets up a disturbance at the level of the signifier (created by the anomalous spelling) which graphically resists such reduction. Its sense remains suspended between the two French verbs 'to differ' and 'to defer', both of which contribute to its textual force but neither of which can fully capture its meaning. Language depends on 'difference' since, as Saussure showed once and for all, it consists in the structure of distinctive oppositions which make up its basic economy. Where Derrida breaks new ground, and where the science of grammatology takes its cue, is in the extent to which 'differ' shades into 'defer'. This involves the idea that meaning is always *deferred*, perhaps to the point of an endless supplementarity, by the play of signification. *Differance* not only designates this theme but offers in its own unstable meaning a graphic example of the process at work.

Derrida deploys a whole rhetoric of similar terms as a means of preventing the conceptual closure – or reduction to an ultimate meaning – which might otherwise threaten his texts. Among them is the notion of 'supplement', itself bound up in a supplementary play of meaning which defies semantic reduction. To see how it is put to work we can turn to Derrida's essays on Rousseau and Lévi-Strauss, where the theme is that of writing in the context of anthropology and the cultural 'sciences of man'.

Culture, nature, writing: Rousseau and Lévi-Strauss

For Derrida, writing (in its extended sense) is at once the source of all cultural activity and the dangerous knowledge of its own constitution which culture must always repress. Writing takes on the subversive character of a 'debased, lateralized, displaced theme', yet one that exercises 'a permanent and obsessive pressure . . . a feared writing must be cancelled because it erases the presence of the self-same (*propre*) within speech' (Derrida 1977a, p. 139). This passage occurs in the course of a chapter on Rousseau, whose *Essay on the Origin of Languages* is the starting-point for one of Derrida's most brilliant meditations.

Rousseau thought of speech as the originary form and the healthiest, most 'natural' condition of language. Writing he regarded with curious distrust as a merely derivative and somehow debilitating mode of expression. This attitude of course falls square with Rousseau's philosophy of human nature, his conviction that mankind had degenerated from a state of natural grace into the bondage of politics and civilized existence. Language becomes an index of the degree to which nature is corrupted and divided against itself by the false sophistications of culture. What Derrida does, in a remarkable tour of argument, is to show that Rousseau contradicts himself at various points in his text, so that far from proving speech to be the origin of language, and writing a merely parasitic growth, his essay confirms the priority of writing and the illusory character of all such myths of origin.

Rousseau, for instance, treats of writing as the 'supplement' of spoken language, existing in a secondary relation to speech just as speech itself – by the same token – is at one remove from whatever it depicts. Such arguments have a long prehistory in Western thought. Like Plato's mystical doctrine of forms, the effect is to devalue the activities of art and writing by constant appeal to a pure metaphysics of presence, their distance from which condemns them to an endless play of deceitful imitation. For Derrida, the 'supplementarity' of writing is indeed the root of the matter, but not in the derogatory sense that Rousseau intended. Writing is the example *par excellence* of a supplement which enters into the heart of all intelligible discourse and comes to define its very nature and condition. Derrida shows that Rousseau's essay submits to this reversal even in the process of condemning the subversive influence he attributes to writing and its 'supplementary' character. A whole strange thematics of the supplement runs through the detail of Rousseau's argument like a guilty obsession and twists his implications against their avowed intent. That Rousseau cannot possibly *mean what he says* (or say what he means) at certain crucial junctures is the outcome of Derrida's perverse but utterly literal reading. Rous-

seau's text, like Saussure's, is subject to a violent wrenching
from within, which prevents it from carrying through the logic
of its own professed intention.

Music was one of the manifold interests which went toward
the Rousseauist philosophy of culture, and Derrida has some
fascinating pages relating Rousseau's ideas on the subject to
the general theme of speech *versus* writing. The argument turns
on Rousseau's preference for the vocal or melodic style, which
he identified with the Italian music of his time, as against the
harmonic or contrapuntal, which typified the supposed weakness and decadence of French tradition. As a matter of musical
history this view is open to all kinds of scholarly question.
Derrida, however, is not concerned so much with musicological
fact as with the *textual* symptoms of doubt and duplicity which
mark Rousseau's argument. The primacy of melody in music is
held to follow from its closeness to song, which in turn represents the nearest approach to the passionate origins of speech
itself. Harmony enters music by the same 'degenerate' process
of supplementarity which marks off writing from speech. As
music developed, melody (as Rousseau explains it) 'impercept-
ibly lost its former energy, and the calculus of intervals was
substituted for nicety of inflection' (quoted in Derrida 1977a,
p. 199).

Derrida fastens upon this and similar passages in Rousseau's
text, and shows that what Rousseau is really describing is the
condition, not of music in a phase of historical decline, but of *any*
music which aspires beyond the stage of a primitive, inarticu-
late cry. Forgetfulness of origin may be the ruse by which
harmony and writing manage to efface the primordial 'warmth'
of a pure communion with nature. Yet Rousseau is forced
obliquely to acknowledge (through the blind-spots and contradictions of his text) that music is strictly *unthinkable* without the
supplement of harmony, or swerve from origin, which marks the
possibility of its progress. Rousseau's 'embarrassment' is
plainest when he attempts to define the orginary nature of
melody and song. If song is already, as Rousseau suggests in his
Dictionary of Music, 'a kind of modification of the human voice',
then how can he assign to it (Derrida asks) 'an absolutely
characteristic (*propre*) modality' (ibid., p. 196)? The text uncon-
sciously confesses what Rousseau is at such pains to deny: that

thought is incapable of positing a pure, unadulterated origin for speech or song. Rousseau's argument, as Derrida describes it,

> twists about in a sort of oblique effort to act *as if* degeneration were not prescribed in the genesis and as if evil *supervened upon* a good origin. As if song and speech, which have the same act and the same birthpangs, had not always already begun to separate themselves. (ibid., p. 199)

Rousseau's text cannot mean what it says, or *literally* say what it means. His intentions are skewed and distorted by the 'dangerous supplement' of writing as it approaches the theme of origin.

Derrida perceives such discrepancies at every turn of Rousseau's argument. Wherever the primacy of 'nature' (or speech) is opposed to the debasements of 'culture' (or writing), there comes into play an aberrant logic which inverts the opposition and cuts away the ground of its very meaning. Thus Rousseau's quest for the 'origin' of language turns out to *presuppose* an already articulate movement of production which must be cut off at source from any such originating presence. The supplement has to be inserted, Derrida writes, 'at the point where language begins to be articulated, is born, that is, from falling short of itself, when its accent or intonation, marking origin and passion within it, is effaced under that *other* mark of origin which is articulation' (ibid., p. 270).

'Accent', 'intonation' and 'passion' are bound up together as positive terms in Rousseau's philosophy of man and nature. They all belong to that ruling ideology of voice-as-presence which equates the primacy of speech with the virtues of an innocent, unclouded self-knowledge. Rousseau constructs an elaborate mythology based on the contrast between 'natural' languages which remain close to their sources in passionate utterance, and 'artificial' languages where passion is overlaid by the rules and devices of convention. The former he associates with 'the South', with a culture largely indifferent to progress and reflecting in its language the gracefulness and innocence of origins. The latter is identified with those 'Northern' characteristics which, for Rousseau, signalize the decadence of progress in culture. Passion is overcome by reason, community life invaded by the forces of large-scale economic order. In language the polarity (according to Rousseau) is equally marked. In the

passionate, mellifluous, vowel-based language of the South
one encounters speech near the well-spring of its origin. The
tongues of the North, by contrast, are marked by a harsh and
heavily *consonantal* structure which makes them more efficient as
communicative instruments but widens the rift between feeling
and meaning, between instinct and expression.

For Derrida, this Rousseauist mythology is a classic instance
of the reasoning that always comes up against its limits in trying
to locate any origin (or 'natural' condition) for language. He
shows how Rousseau associates the threat of writing with that
process of 'articulation' by which language extends its communicative grasp and power. 'Progress' involves a displacement from origin and a virtual supersession of all those elements
in speech – accent, melody, the marks of passion – which bound
language to the speaking individual and community at large.
To deconstruct this mythology of presence, Derrida has only to
pursue that 'strange graphic of supplementarity' which weaves
its way through Rousseau's text. What emerges is the fact that
language, once it passes beyond the stage of a primitive cry, is
'always already' inhabited by writing, or by all those signs of an
'articulate' structure which Rousseau considered decadent. As
with Saussure's linguistic methodology, so with Rousseau's
historical speculation: speech in its imaginary plenitude of
meaning is disrupted at source by the supplement of writing.

This is why Rousseau occupies such a central place in *Of
Grammatology* and Derrida's writing generally. He represents a
whole constellation of themes which, in one form or another,
have dominated subsequent discourse on language and the
'sciences of man'. His texts are a constant, obsessive repetition
of gestures which miss their rhetorical mark and display the
insufficiency of language when it strives for an origin beyond all
reach. The deadlocked prolixity of Rousseau's text is also a
lesson to the modern philosopher or linguist:

> Our language, even if we are pleased to speak it, has already
> substituted too many articulations for too many accents, it
> has lost life and warmth, it is already eaten by writing. Its
> accentuated features have been gnawed through by the con-
> sonants.   (ibid., p. 226)

Speech itself is always shot through with the differences and traces of non-present meaning which constitute articulate language. To attempt to 'think the origin' in Rousseau's fashion is therefore to arrive at a paradox which cannot be resolved or surpassed: 'The question is of an originary supplement, if this absurd expression may be risked, totally unacceptable as it is within classical logic.' The supplement is that which both signifies the lack of a 'presence', or state of plenitude for ever beyond recall, and *compensates* for that lack by setting in motion its own economy of difference. It is nowhere present in language but everywhere presupposed by the existence of language as a pre-articulated system. Philosophies that take no account of its activity are thereby condemned (Derrida argues) to a ceaseless repetition of the paradoxes brought to light in his reading of Rousseau.

This critique is extended to the structuralist anthropology of Claude Lévi-Strauss, where Derrida finds the same issues raised in terms of nature versus culture. Lévi-Strauss was among the first to perceive that the insights of structural linguistics could be applied to other 'languages' or signifying systems in the effort to elucidate their underlying codes. This gave rise to what is perhaps the most impressive single achievement of structuralism in its broad-based interpretative mode. Lévi-Strauss rests his analyses of myth and ritual on the conviction that, behind all the surface varieties thrown up by the world's different cultures, there exist certain deep regularities and patterns which reveal themselves to structural investigation. It is a matter of looking beyond their manifest content to the structures of symbolic opposition and sequence that organize these various narratives. At a certain level of abstraction, he argues, it is possible to make out patterns of development and formal relations which cut right across all distinctions of culture and nationality. Myths can then be seen as a problem-solving exercise, adapted to context in various ways but always leading back to the great abiding issues of human existence – mainly the structures of law and taboo surrounding such institutions as marriage, the family, tribal identity, and so forth. The end-point of such analysis may well be to discover, as Lévi-Strauss frequently does, a formula of algebraic power and simplicity to express the logic underlying a dispersed corpus of myths.

Derrida reads Lévi-Strauss as an heir to both Saussure's

'phonocentric' bias and Rousseau's nostalgic craving for origins and presence. The two lines of thought converge in what Derrida shows to be a subtle but weighted dialectic between 'nature' and 'culture'. The phonocentric basis of Lévi-Strauss's method derives, quite explicitly, from the structural linguistics of Saussure and Roman Jakobson. But along with this methodological commitment there is also, according to Derrida, a '*linguistic* and *metaphysical* phonologism which raises speech above writing'. In effect, Lévi-Strauss is seen as performing for modern (structuralist) anthropology the same ambiguous service that Rousseau performed for the speculative science of his day. The nature/culture opposition can be shown to deconstruct itself even as Lévi-Strauss yields to the Rousseauistic dream of an innocent language and a tribal community untouched by the evils of civilization.

Derrida's arguments are largely based on a single brief excerpt – 'The Writing Lesson' – from Lévi-Strauss's book *Tristes Tropiques* (1961). Here the anthropologist sets out to analyse the emergence of writing and its consequences among a tribe (the Nambikwara) whose transition to 'civilization' he describes with undisguised feelings of sadness and guilt. He records how the motives of political power ('hierarchization, the economic function . . . participation in a quasi-religious secret') manifested themselves in the earliest responses to written language. Lévi-Strauss gives expression, like Rousseau, to an eloquent longing for the lost primordial unity of speech-before-writing. He takes upon himself the burden of guilt produced by this encounter between civilization and the 'innocent' culture it ceaselessly exploits. For Lévi-Strauss, the themes of exploitation and writing go naturally together, as do those of writing and violence.

Derrida's answer is not to deny the inherent 'violence' of writing, nor yet to argue that it marks a stage of irreversible advance beyond the 'primitive' mentality. On the one hand he points out that the Nambikwara, on Lévi-Strauss's own evidence, were already subject to a tribal order marked 'with a spectacular violence'. Their social intrigues and rituals of power are in manifest contrast to the retrospective feelings of the anthropologist, who elsewhere presents an idealized picture of their playful and uncorrupted nature. Moreover, as Derrida argues, this suggests that writing is always already a part of social existence, and cannot be dated from the moment when the anthropologist, that guilty spectator, introduced its merely graphic conventions. In truth, there is no such pure 'authenticity' as Lévi-Strauss (like Rousseau) imagines to have been destroyed by the advent of writing in this narrow sense. 'Self-presence, transparent proximity in the face-to-face of countenances . . . this determination of authenticity is therefore classic . . . Rousseauistic but already the inheritor of Platonism' (Derrida 1977a, p. 138). From this point it is possible for Derrida to argue that the violence of writing is there at the outset of all social discourse; that in fact it marks 'the origin of morality as of immorality', the 'non-ethical opening of ethics'.

Thus Derrida's critique of Lévi-Strauss follows much the same path as his deconstructive readings of Rousseau and Saussure. Once again it is a matter of taking a repressed or subjugated theme (that of writing), pursuing its various textual ramifications and showing how these subvert the very order that strives to hold them in check. Writing, for Lévi-Strauss, is an instrument of oppression, a means of *colonizing* the primitive mind by allowing it to exercise (within due limits) the powers of the oppressor. In Derrida's reading this theme of lost innocence is seen as a romantic illusion and a last, belated showing of the Rousseauist mystique of origins. 'Writing' in Lévi-Strauss's sense is a merely derivative activity which always supervenes upon a culture already 'written' through the forms of social existence. These include the codes of naming, rank, kinship and other such systematized constraints. Thus the violence described by Lévi-Strauss presupposes, 'as the space of its possibility, the violence of the arche-writing, the violence of difference, of classification, and of the system of appellations' (ibid., p. 110).

This latter has to do with the function of *names* in Nambikwara society, their significance and mode of designation. Lévi-Strauss offers a casual anecdote about some children who took out their private animosities by each revealing the other's name in a round of mutual revenge. Since the Nambikwara, according to Lévi-Strauss, place strict prohibitions on the use of proper names, this episode becomes symbolic of the violence that intrudes upon preliterate cultures when their language gives way to promiscuous exchange (or writing). Derrida counters with evidence – again from Lévi-Strauss's own text – that these were *not*, in fact, 'proper names' in the sense the anecdote requires, but were already part of a 'system of appellation' – a social arrangement – which precludes the idea of personal possession. The term 'proper name' is itself improper, so the argument runs, because it carries an appeal to authentic, individuated selfhood. What is really involved is a system of classification, a *designated* name which belongs to the economy of socialized 'difference' and not to the private individual. In this instance, what is prohibited by the Nambikwara is not the breach of any personal rights but rather the utterance of 'what *functions* as the proper name':

> The lifting of the interdict, the great game of the denunciation
> . . . does not consist in revealing proper names, but in tearing
> the veil hiding a classification . . . the inscription within a
> system of linguistico-social differences.   (ibid., p. 111)

Derrida's strategies are most clearly on view in these pages devoted to Lévi-Strauss. The 'nature' which Rousseau identifies with a pure, unmediated speech, and Lévi-Strauss with the dawn of tribal awareness, betrays a nostalgic mystique of presence which ignores the self-alienating character of *all* social existence. Writing again becomes the pivotal term in an argument that extends its implications to the whole prehistory and founding institutions of society.

Moreover, the evidence pointing to this conclusion is *there* in the texts of Lévi-Strauss, as it was in the writings of Rousseau and Saussure. It is not some novel and ultra-sophisticated 'method' of reading devised to keep criticism one jump ahead. Nor does it impinge from outside and above, like certain forms of Marxist criticism which treat 'the text' as a handy support for their own superior knowledge of its meaning or mode of production. (I shall return to this topic at a later point.) Indeed, one of the myths or metaphysical ruses Derrida often attacks is the notion that writing is somehow *external* to language, a threat from outside which must always be countered by the stabilizing presence of speech. Carried down through a long tradition, from Plato to Saussure, this idea is most visibly (and paradoxically) inscribed in the Rousseauistic leanings of Lévi-Strauss. Writing becomes an exteriorized agency of violence and corruption, constantly menacing the communal values so closely identified with speech. Derrida's aim to is to show that, on the contrary, writing emerges both within the very *theme* of speech and within the *text* which strives to realize and authenticate that theme. Deconstruction is in this sense the active accomplice of a repressed but already articulate writing. In Derrida's much-quoted phrase, 'Il n'y a pas de hors-texte' ('There is nothing outside the text').

3
From voice to text:
Derrida's critique of philosophy

It should be clear by now why Derrida attaches such importance to the task of freeing structuralism from Saussure's phonocentric approach. The human voice is the ultimate sanction of
all philosophies – like that of Rousseau – which base themselves
more or less explicitly on a metaphysics of origins and presence.
Among Derrida's first published works was a book on Husserl
(*Speech and Phenomena* 1973) in which he contested the idea that
philosophy could work its way back to a logic of meaning and
experience derived from the immediate data of consciousness
itself. Edmund Husserl (d. 1938) was the virtual founder of
modern phenomenology, a movement of thought to which
Derrida is much indebted, although his debt takes the form (as
usual) of a thorough critique and rewriting of its premisses. I
shall later have various detailed points to make about this
crucial encounter, in which Derrida stakes out the ground for
his deconstructive project. At this point, however, it may be
more useful to state the central issue in terms of my discussion so
far.

Phenomenology sets out to isolate those structures of experience and judgement which cannot be doubted or called into
question by even the most sceptical mind. Husserl believed that
the only valid foundation for knowledge was an attitude that
accepted nothing on trust, rigorously suspending or 'bracketing' all ideas and assumptions that might be products of

delusion. This 'bracketing' of experience would then provide the basis for a philosophy secure in its grasp of the world and immune from the ravages of scepticism. Husserl thought this project all the more vital in view of the self-doubting mood which had overtaken many branches of philosophy towards the end of the last century. A gap had opened up between the 'hard' sciences (those based on experiment and factual observation) and other fields of thought where *interpretative* method played a greater role. This rift was further widened by the naïve or unreflective positivism which had begun to get a hold on philosophy itself. New systems of logic were being devised which, for all their explanatory power, lacked any grounding in the self-conscious process of thought. Unless the mind could arrive at such conclusions by reflecting on the process that produced them – by establishing, that is, an account of its own logical working – philosophy would still be a prey to sceptical doubt. For Husserl, this divorce between knowledge and reflection was approaching a crisis-point which threatened not only the human sciences but the entire project of Western thought (see Husserl 1970). Hence his attempt to provide philosophy with a new rationale which would avoid the twin perils of an unreflecting objectivity and a mere retreat into irrationalism.

The technicalities of Husserl's undertaking need not concern us here. What has to be grasped is the fact that his philosophy denies any resort to mere subjectivism, even while appealing to the 'transcendental ego' (or reflective self-awareness) as an ultimate guarantee. Husserl wanted to demonstrate once and for all that such a ground of appeal was possible *without* abandoning philosophy to the whims of subjective introspection. This called for a firm distinction between those acts of consciousness which defined the very nature of thought and perception, and that other realm of private-individual psychology which offered no such hold for understanding. What Husserl called the process of 'phenomenological reduction' was precisely this endeavour to separate the basic, constitutive structures of perception from the mass of indeterminate or 'merely' subjective experience. In short, Husserl revived for modern philosophy the project of thought which Descartes had initiated three centuries earlier: that of re-establishing the certitudes of reason by systematically doubting everything that could be doubted.

Descartes discovered his own indubitable truth in the thinking subject whose existence in the act of thought was (to his mind) beyond all question. Even *that* residual certainty has since been attacked (by the structuralists, among others) for its confusions of linguistic and logical statement. Husserl's main object was to break this charmed circle of consciousness by showing how the mind took possession of experience, relating thought to the object-of-thought through an act of structured perception. Thinking no longer takes place in a solipsistic realm of reflection cut off from the reality it vainly strives to grasp. Philosophy is reconstructed on the pared-down but firm foundations of a knowledge in and of the world.

What Derrida fastens on to in Husserl's various texts is the element of subjectivism which he sees still at work once the 'transcendental reduction' has been carried through. Husserl himself was far from consistent in explaining just how far the process needed to be taken if the charge of psychologism was to be rebutted, and philosophy placed on a new and firm footing. His early work admitted certain phenomena of consciousness which could well be regarded as belonging more to individual psychology than to any universal structure of mind. In later texts Husserl strove to purge these elements by insisting more rigorously on the 'transcendental' nature of phenomenological reflection. The mind whose operations are experienced and analysed is *not*, he reiterates, the 'empirical' or pre-reflective ego of everyday awareness. It is a form of conscious self-surveillance critically trained upon its own logical workings and thus re-deemed from the errors and uncertainties of common mental experience. For Derrida, however, the question remains whether Husserl was *able* to break so completely with presuppositions which – in one form or another – have dominated the whole of Western intellectual tradition.

His argument turns (as one might expect) on Husserl's treatment of the relation between language and thought. Phenomenology is seen to derive its sense of purpose from the intimate relation assumed to exist between consciousness (or self-presence) and linguistic expression. Husserl draws a cardinal distinction between two kinds of sign, the 'indicative' and the 'expressive'. The latter alone is endowed with meaning (*Bedeutung*) in Husserl's sense of the word, since it represents the communicative purpose or intentional force which 'animates' language. Indicative signs, by contrast, are devoid of expressive intent and function merely as 'lifeless' tokens in a system of arbitrary sense. We have already seen how Derrida set about dismantling a similar opposition in the texts of Rousseau and Lévi-Strauss. In their case the argument was cast in terms of speech versus writing, the former endowed with all the metaphorical attributes of life and healthy vitality, the latter with dark connotations of violence and death. Derrida finds the same powerful metaphors at work in Husserl's meditations on language and thought. 'Indicative' signs are banished to a region of exterior darkness, as remote as possible from the life-giving sources of language. Like Rousseau's feared and disruptive 'writing', they seem to threaten the self-presence of speech by wrenching it away from origin into an endless play of unmotivated, random sense.

Derrida contests this priority by showing once again how the privileged term is held in place by the force of a dominant *metaphor*, and not (as it might seem) by any conclusive logic.

> Although spoken language is a highly complex structure, always containing *in fact* an indicative stratum, which, as we shall see, is difficult to confine within its limits, Husserl has nonetheless reserved for it the power of expression exclusively – and thereby pure logicality.   (Derrida 1973, p. 18)

This latter connection – the link between 'expression' and 'pure logicality' – is crucial to Husserl's undertaking. He seeks to provide a new grounding for logic, not as a self-contained system of axiomatic truths, but as a structure built up from acts of consciousness which grasp the necessity of their own production. Thus logic itself belongs to the expressive (or 'meaningful') activity of thought, as opposed to any purely formal dimension. For Husserl this implies a further distinction between reasoning that is genuinely possessed of its own productive nature and other modes of thought which merely take over an existing methodology.

Behind this opposition, once again, is the idea that consciousness can be fully *authentic* only when its workings express the present activity of a human subject. And from this point, as Derrida shows, it is no great distance to the metaphors of voice and self-presence which govern traditional philosophy. Expression as the 'breath' or 'soul' of meaning, and language as the mere physical 'body' which it comes to animate – such are the covert figurative ploys of Husserlian phenomenology. But, as Derrida argues,

> although there is no expression or meaning without speech, on the other hand not everything in speech is 'expressive'. Although discourse would not be possible without an expressive core, one could almost say that the totality of speech is caught up in an indicative web. (ibid., p.31)

This disturbing possibility – that 'expression' may be tainted at root by the encroachments of 'indicative' meaning – is enough to shake the whole edifice of Husserl's thought.

The term *differance* plays a major dislocating role in the deconstruction of Husserlian themes. It is first introduced by way of describing those elements of non-intended signification which point to a domain of 'indicative' sense beyond the grasp of conscious reflection. Derrida's logic is simple but devastating. Language can fulfil the condition of self-present meaning only if it offers a *total and immediate* access to the thoughts that occasioned its utterance. But this is an impossible requirement. We simply cannot have what Derrida calls 'a primordial intuition of the other's lived experience'. In which case, following Husserl's own distinction, it has to be admitted that language must always fail to achieve expressive self-presence, and must always partake of the indicative character which marks, for Husserl, the suspension of meaning. This may be, according to traditional prejudice, 'the process of death at work in signs'. But that tradition has nothing to fall back upon once its underlying motives and metaphors have thus been questioned. 'Whenever the immediate and full presence of the signified is concealed, the signifier will be of an indicative nature' (ibid., p. 40). And this, as Derrida goes on to argue, is not just a local aberration but a defining characteristic of all uses of language, written or spoken.

Differance thus comes into play (as it did in the essay on Saussure) at the point where meaning eludes the grasp of a pure, self-present awareness. The idea of a temporal *deferring* is also made explicit in relation to Husserl's phenomenology. His quest for a grounding philosophy of conscious experience required that Husserl gave some account of *time* and its various modalities. This was the topic of his book *The Phenomenology of Internal Time-Consciousness* (first published in 1929), in which Husserl set out to analyse the different relations and levels of intelligible order which 'made sense' of time for the experiencing mind (see Husserl 1964). From the phenomenological standpoint, this involved showing how the 'living present' of awareness is the privileged point from which memories, both long- and short-term, are organized and given their due sequential meaning. Among Husserl's most important distinctions is that between *retention* and *representation*, the former having to do with immediate (sensory) traces, the latter with experiences recalled over a greater distance of time. It is here that Derrida inserts the deconstructive lever of *differance*. He points out that Husserl is constantly obliged, by the logic of his own argument, to treat the present as a moment compounded of manifold retentions and anticipations, never existing in the isolated instant of awareness. Time is an endless deferring of presence which drives yet another paradoxical wedge into the project of phenomenology.

This brings about the virtual collapse of all those distinctions Husserl set up in order to preserve the 'living present' in its privileged position. 'Representation' can no longer be distinguished from 'retention', since both are involved in the same ceaseless movement of temporal distancing. What separates them is not the 'radical difference' which Husserl wanted between 'perception and non-perception'; it is, rather, 'a difference between two modifications of non-perception'. In other words, there is no privileged ground of reflection from which thought could ever organize or control the flux of temporal experience. Husserl's main object was to separate perception from representation in such a way that the latter – the realm of 'mediated' signs and impressions – should not interfere with the primary self-evidence of knowledge. What his text in fact reveals, against its own intention, is the 'movement of differance' which always inhabits 'the pure actuality of the now'. This movement undermines Husserl's phenomenology in the same way that writing questions and subverts the privilege of speech. Perception is always already representation, just as speech presupposes (and wills itself to forget) the *differance* of writing.

Phenomenology and/or structuralism?

Derrida is as far from 'rejecting' Husserl as he is from simply dismissing the linguistics of Saussure or the structural anthropology of Lévi-Strauss. In the texts of all three he discovers a set of paradoxical themes, at odds with their manifest argument, which opens them up to a deconstructive reading. On the other hand, these texts are selected precisely for the rigour and tenacity with which they raise the questions that Derrida wishes to press. That the pressure is brought to bear in ways Derrida can twist, so to speak, against their own intentions is not to be taken as wholly undermining their project. This issue came up in the course of an interview with Julia Kristeva (reprinted in the volume *Positions*, translated 1981). What exactly was the status of deconstructive 'method'? Did it hold out any notion of a 'truth' denied to the texts it called into question? How – more pointedly – could Derrida square his vigilant mistrust of metaphysical language with the fact that he had to work, of necessity, *within* that language, even while claiming to dismantle its whole conceptual structure?

Derrida replied characteristically by turning the question round to reveal its oversimplified terms of argument. If there is no possibility of breaking altogether with Western metaphysics, it is equally the case that every text belonging, however rootedly, to that tradition bears within itself the disruptive potential of a deconstructive reading. As Derrida puts it, 'in every proposition or in every system of semiotic research . . . metaphysical presuppositions coexist with critical motifs' (Derrida 1981, p. 36). Deconstruction is therefore an activity performed by texts which in the end have to acknowledge their own partial complicity with what they denounce. The most rigorous reading, it follows, is one that holds itself provisionally open to further deconstruction of its own operative concepts.

This is why Derrida returns so often to writers like Husserl whose texts are problematic in ways that defy any settled or definitive reading. They make it possible to define more exactly the point at which thought encounters an *aporia* – or self-engendered paradox – beyond which it cannot press. This term is used frequently by Derrida and those of his more rigorous disciples, such as Paul de Man, who pursue deconstruction to its furthest bounds of possibility. The *Oxford English Dictionary* rather sidesteps the problem of a worked-out definition but does offer two early instances – both from rhetorical handbooks – which convey something of the suspicion and unease evoked by the word. Puttenham, in his *English Poesie* (1589), refers to 'Aporia, or the Doubtfull. So called . . . because oftentimes we will seem to cast perills, and make doubt of things when by a plaine manner of speech wee might affirme or deny him.' Less moralistic but equally perplexed is an entry from 1657: 'Aporia is a figure whereby the speaker sheweth that he doubteth, either where to begin for the multitude of matters, or what to do or say in some strange ambiguous thing.' Clearly the concept of *aporia* occupied a suspect, even sinister, place in the system of traditional rhetoric. These entries give more than a hint of the unsettling uses to which it will be put in the rhetoric of deconstruction.

Aporia derives from the Greek word meaning 'unpassable path', a sense that fully lives up to its later paradoxical development. In Derrida's hands it represents the nearest one can get to a label or conceptual cover-term for the effects of *differance* and the 'logic' of deviant figuration. What deconstruction persistently reveals is an ultimate impasse of thought engendered by a rhetoric that always insinuates its own textual workings into the truth claims of philosophy. To pursue these workings is to glimpse the possibility of reversing philosophy's age-old repression of writing. This would give rise, in Derrida's words, to a 'writing within which philosophy is inscribed as a place within a system which it does not command'. But this prospect can be grasped only momentarily, in the process of engaging with texts that remain – like the deconstructive project itself – inseparably tied to Western philosophy. Within Derrida's writing there runs a theme of utopian longing for the textual 'free play' which would finally break with the instituted wisdom of language. It is a theme that emerges to anarchic effect in some of his later texts (to which I shall return in subsequent pages). For the most part, however, Derrida argues that deconstruction must 'bore from within', or work to dismantle the texts of philosophy with concepts borrowed from philosophy itself.

This reciprocal dependence is nowhere more evident than in Derrida's relationship to Husserl. In his essay 'Genesis and Structure' (in Derrida 1978), he attempts to locate the moment of suspense or hesitation where Husserl is faced with an *impossible* choice between two equally 'valid' but mutually exclusive schemes of explanation. These schemes are, broadly speaking, phenomenological and structuralist. The one seeks to account for knowledge and experience by offering a 'genetic' explanation of how the mind (the 'transcendental ego' of Husserlian parlance) constitutes its own reality. The other eschews such a method – suspecting it, perhaps, of some complicity with subjectivism – and turns instead to the notion of 'structure' as an ultimate guarantee. These two dimensions of thought are the poles between which Husserl has to steer if his project is not to be captured by uncritical motives and themes.

And this, Derrida argues, is a problem not only for Husserlian phenomenology but for all philosophical thinking which penetrates beyond a certain level of awareness. Subjectivism is not the only trap philosophy has to avoid. Structuralism has its own special dangers, the nature of which Husserl was quicker to grasp than most of its present-day practitioners. The concept of structure (as we have already seen) can easily be *immobilized* by assuming it to possess some kind of 'objective' or self-validating status. In this sense it is possible to argue, like Derrida, that 'a certain structuralism has always been philosophy's most spontaneous gesture'. The explanatory props of 'structure' are always available when thought tries to ignore the question of how its own regulative concepts are brought into play. What Husserl shows up, albeit fitfully, is the gap (or *aporia*) between structuralism in its objectivist guise and everything that cannot be accounted for in structuralist terms. His entire undertaking is an effort to reconcile two different orders of thought which can never be reduced to each other's terms but which none the less cannot be assumed to exist in self-sufficient isolation. The 'structuralist' quest, as Derrida reads it, is always for 'a form or function organized according to an internal legality in which elements have meaning only in the soldarity of their correlation or their opposition' (ibid., p. 157). The 'genetic' demand, on the other hand, is 'the search for the origin and the foundation of the structure'. In *Speech and Phenomena* the object had been mainly to deconstruct such ideas of 'origin' and 'foundation' by showing them to be always already inscribed in a differential structure of meaning. In 'Genesis and Structure' the argument is angled, not from the opposite side, but from a larger perspective which admits the necessity of both (irreducible) systems of thought.

Derrida's critique of structuralism is continued in the essay 'Force and Signification', which likewise questions the internal self-sufficiency of a theory given over to system and concept. Structuralism always asserts itself where thinking yields to the attractions of order and stability. Its achievements, however impressive, are intrinsically limited to 'a reflection of the accomplished, the constituted, the *constructed*' (Derrida 1978, p. 5). What is suppressed by this static conceptualization is the 'force' or animating pressure of intent which exceeds all the bounds of structure.

Derrida here seems remarkably close to Husserl's insistence on the life-giving content of 'expression', which redeems signs from the fixity of dead convention. He goes so far as to compare the results of structuralist analysis with a city laid waste by some mysterious 'catastrophe' of nature. But the point of these metaphors is not to reinstate a thematics of presence or expression, as opposed to the *différance* of structural inscription. Rather, it is to demonstrate that structuralism itself arises from the break with an attitude (the phenomenological) it cannot reject but must perpetually put in question. The concept of structure is wrenched from within by denying it its conceptual status and showing how it functions as a *metaphor* to contain the unruly energies of meaning. Structuralism and phenomenology are locked in a reciprocal *aporia* from which neither can emerge with its principles intact, but on which both depend for their moments of maximum insight.

Conventional accounts of modern French criticism tend to reduce this relationship between phenomenology and structuralism to a matter of successive 'schools' or waves of interest. Structuralism, it is assumed, grew out of phenomenology and then, in the other sense of the phrase, 'grew out' of it – rejected its assumptions and developed an alternative basis of theory. This idea is plausible up to a point. Phenomenology certainly helped to lay the ground for structuralism by focusing attention more keenly on the ways in which consciousness perceives and makes sense of the world. It offered a philosophy of language where the idea of structure was already implicit, since meaning was seen as a productive interplay between the text and the reader's quest for intelligibility. Where it differed from structuralism was in the assumption (following Husserl) that meaning was always a kind of creative *excess*, surpassing any possible account of its origin based on the notion of structure.

Maurice Merleau-Ponty, Husserl's most distinguished successor, states the issue with perfect clarity. Language – and speech in particular – represents

> that paradoxical operation through which, by using words of a given sense, and already available meanings, we try to follow up an *intention* which necessarily outstrips, modifies and in the last analysis stabilizes the meanings of the words which translate it.   (Merleau-Ponty 1962, p. 389)

According to this view, language in its 'creative' uses outruns what might be accounted for in terms of purely 'structured' or pre-existent meaning. Contrary to structuralist thinking, it reveals an 'excess of the signified over the signifying' which places it beyond all reach of reductive explanations.

This theme of the creative or intentional 'surplus' in meaning goes a long way to explain the rift between structuralism and phenomenology. The activating principle of structuralist thought, at least in its earlier manifestations, was precisely the *refusal* to acknowledge any meaning outside or beyond the constraints of a pre-existent language. Yet it is not hard to see how a dialogue might now be reopened between phenomenology and the post-structuralist themes of text, writing and deconstruction. Merleau-Ponty himself seems to move in this direction – as is apparent if one looks more closely at some of his later essays, especially those collected in the volume *Signs* (1964). Merleau-Ponty's reflections persistently dwell on the sheer *impossibility* of distinguishing 'structure' from 'meaning', or expression from that which precedes it and makes it possible. Language, he suggests at one point, can only be conceived of as 'a surpassing of the signifying by the signified which it is the very virtue of the signifying to make possible' (Merleau-Ponty 1964, p. 90). In its sense of an irreducibly two-way dependence, this description marks a definite shift from Merleau-Ponty's earlier position. It acknowledges the claims of structure while still holding on to the necessity of thinking beyond their more rigid application.

The point is made most tellingly in an essay on Matisse, occasioned by a documentary film of the artist at work. It would be wrong, Merleau-Ponty suggests, to 'believe' in what the film portrays as an inspired but at the same time *premeditated* build-up to the finishing stroke. By a simple gesture Matisse is made to resolve 'the problem which in retrospect seemed to imply an infinite number of data'. The process of creation is unthinkable in terms which insist on the simplified either/or of expressive versus structural description. Rather, as Merleau-Ponty carefully phrases it,

> the chosen line was chosen in such a way as to observe, scattered out over the painting, twenty conditions which were unformulated and even informulable for anyone but Matisse, since they were only defined and imposed by the intention of executing *this painting which did not yet exist*.   (ibid., p. 46)

This manages to state, more clearly than any abstract account, the paradox Merleau-Ponty discovers at the heart of language and all signifying systems. The 'surpassing' of structure by meaning cannot be described simply in terms of subjective 'intention'. Merleau-Ponty is at one with the structuralists in seeing that meaning is always necessarily inscribed in a pre-existent economy of sense which it can never fully control. On the other hand, he shows that this very condition, by creating such a complex background of constraints, makes it possible for meaning to emerge in new and unforeseeable ways. Merleau-Ponty's later philosophy is a constant search for that 'fecund moment' when meaning discovers the structure which will 'make it manageable for the artist and at the same time accessible to others'.

It is this same ultimate paradox that structuralism approaches, so to speak, from the opposite side. Where Merleau-Ponty finds meaning perpetually on the brink of investing itself

with structure, Barthes would see structures endlessly producing new possibilities of sense. Derrida is pointing to a similar
moment of convergence in his essays on structuralism and
phenomenology. By deconstructing the play of concept and
metaphor behind these two philosophies, Derrida arrives at his
own formulation of the problems encountered by Merleau-
Ponty. Structuralism lives on what he calls 'the difference
between its promise and its practice'. The practice has mostly
given way to those enticing metaphors, derived from structural
linguistics, which elevate 'form' at the expense of 'force', or
structure to the detriment of what goes on *within* and *beyond*
structure. The 'promise' survives in that other, self-critical
strain of structuralist thought which implicitly questions its
own methodical grounding. There is always, according to
Derrida, an 'opening' which baffles and frustrates the structuralist project. 'What I can never understand, in a structure, is
that by means of which it is not closed' (Derrida 1978, p. 160).
Hence the importance of Husserlian phenomenology as an
intimate running critique of structuralist thought. What
Husserl powerfully demonstrates, often against his immediate
intention, is 'the principled, essential, and structural impossibility of closing a structural phenomenology' (ibid.).

Derrida's sights are thus firmly set against the idea that
structuralism has brought about a total and irreversible break
with its own prehistory. This heady delusion – still current in
some quarters of the structuralist Left – ignores the dangers of
pre-emptive closure and conceptual rigidity which Derrida
brings to light. It would also be wrong, and for much the same
reason, to regard deconstruction as 'post-structuralist' in the
sense of displacing or invalidating the structuralist project.
Without that specific tension between 'practice' and 'promise'
exemplified in structuralist thought, Derrida could hardly have
broached the questions that animate his own writing. Deconstruction is a constant and vigilant reminder of what structuralism *must be* if it is to avoid the traps laid down by its seductive
concepts of method.

By virtue of its innermost intention, and like all questions
about language, structuralism escapes the classical history of
ideas which already presupposes structuralism's possibility,

for the latter naïvely belongs to the province of language and
propounds itself within it.   (ibid., p.4)

This 'innermost intention' is the aspect of structuralist thinking
which eludes methodical reduction and which Derrida strives to
maintain. Otherwise – as he shows most clearly in the case of
Saussure – structuralism is destined simply to rejoin the tradition it promised to transform.

4
Nietzsche:
philosophy and deconstruction

Friedrich Nietzsche (1844–1900) remains for most modern philosophers what he was for his contemporaries: a scandal wrapped in layers of enigma. One reaction in recent times has been to brand him as a dire precursor of the Nazi phenomenon, a thinker whose supposedly 'irrationalist' outlook and megalomaniac pretensions paved the way for Hitler and his ideologues. These charges cannot be altogether rejected. They rest on a partial reading of Nietzsche which was actively encouraged by certain of his followers and no doubt exercised some baleful influence, if not on the scale imagined by his latter-day detractors. Suffice it to say that Nietzsche's doctrinaire mythology, his ideas of the 'superman' and 'eternal recurrence', have suffered considerable guilt by association.

But alongside these writings Nietzsche also conducted a critique of Western philosophy and its presuppositions which has lost nothing of its power to provoke and disturb. It is this aspect of Nietzsche's thought which has left its mark on the theory and practice of deconstruction. To speak of 'influence' here would be somewhat misleading, since the word implies a handing-down of concepts and themes as if within a centralized tradition of authority. What Derrida brings out, after all, is the way in which writing exceeds all the various proprietory claims laid down by the conventional 'history of ideas'. If texts are unbounded by authorial intent and open to radical deconstruction, then clearly there is no question of Derrida's having simply absorbed Nietzsche's influence and put his ideas to work in a modern, post-structuralist context. What Nietzsche provides, on the contrary, is a *style* of philosophic writing which remains intensely sceptical of all claims to truth – its own included – and which thus opens up the possibility of liberating thought from its age-old conceptual limits.

Nietzsche is not to be taken at his own self-estimate, as having once and for all put a close to the deluded quest of Western metaphysics. Like Saussure or Husserl, he remains to some extent a prisoner of the themes and rooted conventions of thought which his writing begins to question. These themes, as Derrida so often reminds us, run deep in the logic and communicative structure of language, so deep indeed that to break with them entirely would be to risk madness or total non-communication. (Nietzsche himself was declared insane and produced nothing more than random, unintelligible jottings during the last sixteen years of his life.) More than any philosopher in the Western tradition, Nietzsche pressed up against those limits of language and thought which Derrida attempts to define. He anticipates the style and strategy of Derrida's writing to a point where the two seem often engaged in a kind of uncanny reciprocal exchange.

The reasons for this are not far to seek. Nietzsche often seems to spell out in advance the programme and systematic ruses of deconstruction, adopting the same attitude of sceptical rigour and denying himself any secure resting-place in method or concept. Philosophers, he argued, were the self-condemned dupes of a 'truth' which preserved itself simply by effacing the *metaphors*, or figurative discourse, which brought it into being. If language is radically metaphorical, its meanings (as Saussure was later to show) caught up in an endless chain of relationship and difference, then thought is deluded in its search for a truth beyond the mazy detours of language. Only by suppressing its origins in metaphor had philosophy, from Plato to the present, maintained the sway of a tyrannizing reason which in effect denied any dealing with figural language. Reason had crushed out the imaginative life of philosophy, just as – in Nietzsche's view – it had destroyed the joyous or 'Dionysian' element in classical Greek tragedy. Socrates stands – with Christ in

Nietzsche's inverted pantheon – as the pale destroyer of all that gives life, variety and zest to the enterprise of human understanding. To restore that buried tradition is to show how 'reason' usurped its place by systematically opposing and disguising the rhetorical gambits of language.

An arresting image from Nietzsche conveys the extent of his scepticism about knowledge and truth. What remains of such notions, Nietzsche asks, once we have seen through the twists and displacements by which language simultaneously hides and perpetuates its own devious workings? Truth, he concludes,

> is a mobile marching army of metaphors, metonymies and anthropomorphisms . . . truths are illusions of which one has forgotten that they *are* illusions . . . coins which have their obverse effaced and which are no longer of value as coins but only as metal . . . (quoted by Spivak, in Derrida 1977a, p. xxii)

For Nietzsche this insight led to the conclusion that *all* philosophies, whatever their claim to logic or reason, rested on a shifting texture of figurative language, the signs of which were systematically repressed under the sovereign order of Truth. This bottomless relativity of meaning, and the ways in which philosophers have disguised or occluded their ruling metaphors, are the point of departure for Derrida's writing like Nietzsche's before him.

Of course there are plenty of precedents for the idea that language is radically metaphorical in character. The doctrine took shape among the German Romantics, and passed down through Coleridge to modern critics like I. A. Richards, whose *Philosophy of Rhetoric* (1936) expounded what might seem an uncompromising line on the central importance of metaphor. 'Thought is metaphoric,' Richards declared, 'and the metaphors of language derive therefrom.' In contesting the traditional view of metaphor (that it is merely a grace or incidental supplement of language), and in thus reversing an entrenched priority, Richards goes some way towards the deconstructionist outlook. The difference appears when he proposes that 'to improve the theory of metaphor' we must 'take more notice of the skill in thought which we possess' and 'translate more of our skill into discussable science' (Richards 1936, p. 116). There is still the implication, despite Richards's high claims for metaphor, that a 'science' or logical meta-language exists which can step outside the figural domain and survey its peculiar contours.

This assumption runs deep in Richards's thinking, as it does across virtually the entire domain of modern Anglo-American philosophy and criticism. In his early writings Richards put forward an 'emotive' theory of poetic language, in terms of which poetry could be valued for its powers of evocative and life-enhancing metaphor, while escaping the rigid truth-conditions of logical-positivist philosophy. His distinction was seized upon by the American New Critics, and became (as we have seen) the basis of their various rhetorical schemes of explanation. A gulf was thus fixed between poetry and rational knowledge, a no-man's-land which permitted no crossing except by a strict observance of the saving and peculiar 'logic' of figurative language. Structuralism in its early, scientistic guise was subject to the same general ordinance. Criticism aspired to the condition of a metalanguage or encompassing theory of the text which derived its explanatory power from precisely this sense of disciplined objectivity.

Derrida follows the Nietzschean lead in his break with this self-accrediting notion of method and validity. 'Science', in Derrida's usage, is a discourse linked to the repressive ideology of reason, which in turn (as Nietzsche argued) took rise from the Greek equation between truth and logic. What is in question, for Nietzsche and Derrida, is not some 'alternative' logic of figurative language but an open plurality of discourse where all such priorities dissolve into the disconcerting 'free play' of signs. Derrida writes (in his essay 'Structure, Sign and Play') of the two 'interpretations of interpretation' which between them stake out the region traversed by modern debates on language and method. Both are 'structuralist' in the extended sense of the term which, as we have seen, Derrida applies to a long and diverse tradition of Western thought. They are both concerned, that is to say, with interpreting the means by which thought makes sense of an otherwise inchoate experience. Where they differ is in the degree of order and stability imposed by their respective quests for meaning. On the one hand is the attitude –

exemplified here by Lévi-Strauss – which clings to the concept of structure as a refuge from the giddying motions of pure *differance*. On the other is posed the more radical choice, that which involves, as Derrida describes it, 'the Nietzschian *affirmation* . . . of the play of the world and of the innocence of becoming . . . of a world of signs without fault, without truth, and without origin which is offered to an active interpretation' (Derrida 1978, p. 292). It is this dimension of Nietzsche's thought which has not merely 'influenced' but in many ways uncannily pre-empted the work of deconstruction.

Nietzsche, Plato and the sophists

Nietzsche's critique of philosophy was as far-reaching in its historical scope as in the zest with which it set out to attack all current conventions of knowledge. It involved a full-scale 'genealogy' of Western morality and thought, a diagnostic survey which worked right back to the Greek foundations of reason itself. For Nietzsche it seemed that this tradition had been firmly set on course by the style of dialectical argument invented by Socrates and passed on through the texts of his student Plato. The dialectical method of eliciting 'truth' from a carefully contrived encounter of wisdom and ignorance was – according to Nietzsche – no more than a rhetorical ploy. Its persuasiveness, however, was such as to monopolize for itself all claims to reason, dignity and truth. As a result, philosophy renounced all dealing with rhetoric and looked upon the arts of language (especially writing) as sources of error and delusion. Among the contemporary targets of Socratic disdain was the school of rhetorician-philosophers known as the sophists, a name that still connotes – as it did for Plato – verbal ingenuity mixed with persuasive guile. Socrates is shown running circles of argument round one of their number in Plato's dialogue *The Gorgias*. Here dialectic wins out, as always, by placing its questions with strategic skill and forcing the opponent into a position of weakness *on Socrates' terms*. The upshot, crudely summarized, is to demonstrate that rhetoric possesses neither reason nor moral self-knowledge; that its powers of persuasion are ethically indifferent and apt to be indulged in the worst causes.

Nietzsche's response is not to deny the potential aberrations of rhetoric but to argue, on the contrary, that Socrates himself is a wily rhetorician who scores his points by sheer tactical cunning. Behind all the big guns of reason and morality is a fundamental will to persuade which craftily disguises its workings by imputing them always to the adversary camp. Truth is simply the honorific title assumed by an argument which has got the upper hand – and kept it – in this war of competing persuasions. If anything, the sophist comes closer to wisdom by implicitly acknowledging what Socrates has to deny: that thinking is always and inseparably bound to the rhetorical devices that support it.

Deconstruction on two wheels

Nietzsche's transvaluation of philosophy therefore demanded a return to source and an effort to deconstruct the ruling metaphors of reason itself. There is an odd but revealing parallel to this in Robert Pirsig's novel *Zen and the Art of Motorcycle Maintenance* (1974), where the narrative interest has more to do with Greek philosophy than with Zen Buddhism, as many readers have no doubt been puzzled to find. The central figure is a man on the verge of breakdown and despair who sets out on a coast-to-coast motorcycle trip across America in search of self-understanding. What emerges gradually in the course of this quest is a whole buried prehistory of intellectual conflict which – we come to realize – led up to the events of the novel. Through a sequence of dimly remembered episodes the narrator reconstructs a portrait of his own previous life, the last few months of which were spent as a student of philosophy at the University of Chicago. Under the pseudonym 'Phaedrus' – adopted for reasons which soon become clear – this doomed *alter ego* is shown in the process of challenging all the basic assumptions handed down by his teachers on pain of virtual excommunication.

When Phaedrus begins to read back into the sources, especially the texts of Plato and Aristotle, he finds their arguments not only unconvincing but deviously angled in such a way as everywhere to misrepresent their forgotten opponents. The sophists, in particular, are held up to philosophic ridicule by a method of argument which twists their case into a parody of its own just-visible outline. From Socrates down through Plato and Aristotle, the evidence points to a massive suppression and misinterpretation of everything that threatened the sovereign power of dialectical reason.

Phaedrus himself is cast as a latter-day victim of this same 'conspiracy', suffering the taunts of professors and students unwilling to question the wisdom of ages. The 'Church of Reason' is too firmly established in Chicago, with its neo-Aristotelian stress on the virtues of clear-cut logical analysis and firmly categorical thinking. The trouble comes to a head for Phaedrus when his class is taken over – ominously – by the Chairman for the Committee on Analysis of Ideas and Study of Method. What ensues – at least in Phaedrus's inflamed imagination – is an ultimate duel of wits between 'dialectic' and 'rhetoric', with rhetoric decisively winning the day. The turning-point comes with his realization that ' "dialectic" had some special meaning that made it a fulcrum word – one that can shift the balance of an argument, depending on how it's placed'. By challenging the Chairman to explain the provenance of dialectic – its 'genealogy', in Nietzschean terms – Phaedrus shows it to rest on a willed and systematic forgetting of its own rhetorical origins. Reason, or the supposed self-evidence of reason, is thrown into doubt by its manifest failure to justify its methods on other than purely tautological grounds. Hence Phaedrus's triumphant conclusion:

> The halo round the heads of Plato and Socrates is now gone. He sees that they are consistently doing that which they accuse the Sophists of doing – using emotionally persuasive language for the ulterior purpose of making the weaker argument, the case for dialectic, appear the stronger. We always condemn most in others, he thought, that which we most fear in ourselves.   (Pirsig 1974, p. 378)

But that way madness lies. Phaedrus cannot communicate his discovery within the norms of institutionalized knowledge and 'dialogue' so zealously preserved by the Chicago Aristotelians. He leaves the university and suffers (like Nietzsche) a collapse into silence and neurosis.

The 'original' Phaedrus, in Plato's dialogue of that title, is yet another foil for Socrates, a young and vaunting rhetorician whose headlong gambits are neatly anticipated at every turn (see Plato 1973). As far as the latter-day Phaedrus is concerned, this exchange simply follows the standard pattern of an argument ignoring its own complicity with the tricks and devices of which it sternly disapproves. The *Phaedrus* is also, as it happens, a crucial text for Derrida's reading of Greek philosophy. It contains Plato's most vigorous attack upon writing, couched in the same familiar terms – 'presence' versus 'absence', living speech versus the dead letter – as made up the argument of Rousseau's essay. Writing is the dangerous 'supplement' which lures language away from its authentic origins in speech and self-presence. To commit one's thoughts to writing is to yield them up to the public domain, to risk being misconstrued by all the promiscuous wiles of interpretation. Writing is the 'death' that lies in wait for living thought, the subtle agent of corruption whose workings infect the very sources of truth. Plato's case against rhetoric is therefore of a piece with his attitude to writing. Both are seen as the rebellious servant to a master (truth or dialectic) whose authority they flout by setting themselves up as alternative paths to wisdom.

As Pirsig's Phaedrus accounts for it, rhetoric was denatured and deprived of its force through being treated as merely a collection of classified devices, reducible to system and order. Aristotle brought this process to a high point of rational perfection: 'Rhetoric has become an object, and as an object has parts. And the parts have relationships to one another and these relations are immutable' (Pirsig 1974, p. 368). Whence, incidentally, the motorcycle connection: a machine for Phaedrus is more than the sum of its parts as laid out in a service manual.

Curiously enough, the novel never mentions Nietzsche, though its line of philosophical argument is everywhere prompted by a Nietzschean spirit of critique. The crucial question Phaedrus poses – whence the authority of Socratic reason? – is posed and answered by Nietzsche in strikingly similar terms. It is rhetoric, not dialectic, which takes us back furthest toward the origin of thought in man's encounter with experience: 'Dialectic, which is the parent of logic, came itself from rhetoric. Rhetoric is in turn the child of the myths and poetry of ancient Greece' (ibid., p. 391). Phaedrus is thus led back to the pre-Socratic philosophers, those shadowy figures whom Nietzsche admired for having the courage of their own metaphors. These thinkers had identified reality with various elemental forces in the natural world. For Thales the 'immortal principle' was that of water, while Anaximenes varied the metaphor to air, and Heraclitus – the philosopher of change and flux – saw fire as the element of all things. Their 'explanations' were of course a species of poetic analogy, and yield small sense to the rational (or post-Socratic) mind. But, as Phaedrus declares, 'everything is analogy', including the presumptive generalizations involved in dialectical argument. The difference is that the dialectician, unlike his 'irrational' precursor, fails to recognize this operative movement in the process of thought itself.

Writing and philosophy

Deconstruction begins with the same gesture of turning reason against itself to bring out its tacit dependence on another, repressed or unrecognized, level of meaning. Phaedrus's glimpse of how the concept *dialectic* could be used as a 'fulcrum' to achieve this reversal is very much in keeping with Derrida's textual strategies. In his texts on Greek philosophy Derrida traces some of the ruses and devices by which writing is systematically opposed to the themes of truth, self-presence and origin. But *why* this animus towards writing? The likeliest historical explanation, adopted by many scholars, is that writing was a relatively new development at this stage in Greek cultural life, and that Plato tended to mistrust what he saw as its dangerous diffusion of knowledge and power. This argument clearly has much in common with the Nietzschean-Derridean view of Socratic reason as a tyrannizing force of repression. On the other hand it ignores the textual strategies and the deep-grained metaphysics of presence which a deconstructive reading uncovers. For Derrida the suppression of writing is no mere accident of chronology or quirk of a culture in transition. It operates, in Plato and his numerous descendants, through a mode of self-perpetuating rhetoric unglimpsed by the conventional historian of ideas.

That this attitude to writing has remained deeply entrenched can be seen from a text like F. M. Cornford's *Before and After Socrates* (1932), a widely read introduction to Greek philosophy and its background. Cornford shows a kind of condescending patience with the sophists, treating them as adolescent rebels on the way to Socratic wisdom and dignity. When he comes to the relationship between Socrates and Plato, his comments perfectly illustrate the marked devaluation of writing by a powerful mystique of origins. Socrates, according to Cornford, was one of those choice spirits who by 'living the truth' bequeathed an example more potent than any mere text.

> They have divined in our nature unsuspected powers which only they have as yet, in their own persons, brought to fulfilment. . . . Conviction is slowly carried to posterity by the example of their lives, not by any record they bequeath in writing. For, with few exceptions, they have not written books. They were wise, and knew that the letter is destined to kill much (though not all) of the life that the spirit has given.   (Cornford 1932, p. 62)

Nothing could show more clearly the Socratic equation between truth, presence and the primal authority of speech. Without fully endorsing Plato's idea of writing as a childish invention, an affront to mature wisdom, Cornford yet manages to imply that Socrates preserved his truths intact by not having to submit them to the infantile lures of textuality.

Derrida pursues these sanctions against writing deep into the labyrinth of Plato's thought. He discovers a further opposition between 'good' and 'bad' writing, the one envisaged as 'natural' and inscribed upon the soul by the laws of reason, the other a debased and 'literal' script which obtrudes its shadow between truth and understanding. As Derrida shrewdly notes, this distinction is made possible by a *metaphoric* switch wherein the figurative ('good') writing becomes more real and immediate than its literal counterpart. In Christian as in Platonic tradition, the material script is devalued in favour of a spiritual writing imprinted directly on the soul without the aid of material instruments. This 'simulated immediacy' then becomes the source of all authentic wisdom and truth. What cannot be acknowledged within this Platonic scheme is the fact that it depends on a root *metaphor* of writing, one that it strives to repress even while perpetually playing variations on its terms. Deconstruction insists – paradoxically – on the literal status of this otherwise self-supporting metaphor. It is not, as Derrida says, 'a matter of inverting the literal meaning and the figurative meaning but of determining the "literal" meaning of writing as metaphoricity itself' (Derrida 1977a, p. 15). It is here that deconstruction finds its rock-bottom sense of the irreducibility of metaphor, the *differance* at play within the very constitution of 'literal' meaning. It finds, in short, that there *is* no literal meaning.

Greek philosophy is not the only source for this double valuation of 'good' and 'bad' writing. Derrida cites a multiplicity of texts, including those many biblical passages which distinguished the ineffable 'writing' of God – vouchsafed to the soul through divine illumination – from the fallen, material inscriptions of worldly language (see ibid., pp. 16 ff.). By thus creating a twofold order of writing in its 'sensible' and 'intelligible' aspects, theology seconded the Platonist belief in a 'writing of the soul' which had to be protected from the mere physicality of signs. The *logos* of revealed truth, whether Platonist or Christian, harks back to a state of linguistic grace before the 'fall' of language into a mode of debased and corporeal written existence. In medieval theology the two traditions came together: 'the intelligible face of the sign remains turned toward the word and the face of God'.

It is the same distinction between 'sensible' and 'intelligible' orders of meaning which Derrida sets out to deconstruct in the texts of Husserl. Indeed, its effects can be seen, he argues, in every philosophy committed to the notion of a meaning somehow anterior to the signs that serve to convey it. This applies even to Saussure's cardinal distinction between 'signifier' and 'signified', the terms of which – for all their radical potential – remain caught up in a version of Platonic dualism. This bifurcated image of the sign belongs, as Derrida argues,

> to the totality of the great epoch covered by the history of metaphysics, and in a more explicit and a more systematically articulated way to the narrower epoch of Christian creationism and infinitism when these appropriate the resources of Greek conceptuality.   (ibid., p. 13)

Structuralism and semiotics remain a part of this tradition so long as they preserve the Saussurian bar between signifier and signified, 'sensible' token and 'intelligible' concept.

Beyond interpretation?

Yet thought cannot altogether break with this distinction, no matter how rigorously it tries to suspend – or place within brackets – the terms it has to work with. We arrive once again at that Nietzschean-Derridean limit where the only possible way forward is a vigilant textual practice aware of its own meta-physical liabilities. Nietzsche is fully as rigorous as Derrida when it comes to deconstructing his own rhetorical motives and denying himself any claim to consistency of method.

This would seem to raise problems, as I hinted earlier, with those passages where Derrida cites the Nietzschean text in a clearly positive or approving spirit. Such a response can only be at odds with Nietzsche's *tout court* rejection of truth values and his refusal to engage in the kind of interpretative thought that invites further reinterpretation. Nietzsche, on the contrary, permits his reader no such comforting assurance that the 'truth' of his writing is there to be discovered by a careful passage from signifier to signified. To interpret him thus is to fall once again into the great Platonic illusion of a realm of purely intelligible meaning obscured by the material artifice of language. Nietzsche, like Barthes and Derrida, deploys every means of resisting this drift toward interpretation in its various traditional forms. His plurality of styles and cultivation of paradox are strategies intended to arrest understanding, as far as possible, at the level of the text where signification has not yet congealed into meaning or concept. His image of writing as a 'dance of the pen' is one to which Derrida often reverts in order to suggest this free play of sense.

But, again, this seems to take the word for the will in a manner paradoxically opposed to Nietzsche's (and, indeed, Derrida's) way of thinking. How does one begin to interpret a text that denies the very logic of interpretative thought, and hence undercuts the reader's every move to assimilate its meanings into some kind of ordered intelligibility? And – more tellingly from Derrida's standpoint – where can deconstruction find a

hold for interpreting texts that so shrewdly rehearse and anticipate its own Nietzschean call for an end to interpretation?

Nietzsche and Heidegger

These questions are driven to the brink of deliberate absurdity
in Derrida's latest encounter with Nietzsche (*Spurs*, 1979). This
text offers little in the way of 'serious' argumentation, at least of
the kind that most philosophers would accept or know how to
reckon with. It mostly settles for a style of fantastical juggling
with images and wild – even faked – etymologies. The object of
these shuttling tactics is not so much Nietzsche as Heidegger's
influential reading of Nietzsche, an interpretation Derrida regards as both exemplary of its kind and – for precisely that
reason – open to deconstruction. Martin Heidegger (1889–
1976) was a German philosopher who exercised a powerful
influence on modern existentialist and hermeneutic thought.
'Hermeneutics', as Heidegger conceived it, was the founding
philosophy of all interpretation, an attempt to provide the
human sciences with a self-understanding adequate to their
task. For Heidegger this meant a questing back to the origins of
thought and a gradual unveiling of the truth obscured by
centuries of rationalist philosophy. Heidegger's 'influence' on
Derrida is a topic of great complexity which the reader can find
most usefully outlined in Gayatri Chakravorty Spivak's Preface
to the English *Grammatology* (Derrida 1977a). For the moment
we can focus more specifically on Heidegger's critique of
Nietzsche and the way in which Derrida intervenes to disrupt
and reverse its effect.

Heidegger mounts a project of 'hermeneutic' recovery which
aims to interpret the meaning and significance of Nietzsche's
text through a full understanding of the motives and tradition
that produced it. Nietzsche is seen as the last and desperate
spokesman for a Western metaphysics run aground on its
rationalist assumptions, and vainly trying to surmount the
various problems of its own engendering. Nietzsche is a vital
figure in the history of thought because, according to Heidegger, he represents reason up against its limits and incipiently
harking back to a Being, or point of origin, that preceded all the
obfuscating wiles of rationality. That Nietzsche ultimately

failed in this attempt is a sign that he remained partly captive to a system of thought he could only *reject* or *invert*, without seeing back beyond its limiting suppositions. What this would entail, for Heidegger, is a bracketing of all those logical assumptions that inhabit the very grammar and predicative structure of Western thought. Language itself perpetuates the rationalist parcelling-out of experience into categories like 'subject' and 'object', distinctions that obey the analytic drive towards the mastery of nature by reason. To think one's way beyond such categories is to ask, with Heidegger, not *how* things exist but *why* they should exist in the first place. Hence the crucial distinction between 'Being' and 'beings', the former conceived as the ground of existence prior to all knowledge, the latter as the realm of existent entities already marked out by reason.

This gross simplification of Heidegger's thought will perhaps at least serve to bring out its challenging significance for Derrida. Up to a point there is clearly much in common between deconstruction and the Heideggerian project of undoing the conceptual knots and ties implicit in Western philosophy. In each case it is a matter of making do with the language bequeathed by that tradition, while maintaining a rigorous scepticism about its ultimate validity or meaning. Indeed, one of Derrida's most typical strategies for achieving this suspension of concepts comes directly from Heidegger's textual practice. This is the device of placing words *sous rature* or 'under erasure', signified by crossing them through in the text and thus warning the reader not to accept them at philosophic face value. Thus, in *Of Grammatology*: 'the sign is that ill-named thing, the only one, that escapes the instituting question of philosophy' (Derrida 1977a, p. 19). The marks of erasure acknowledge both the *inadequacy* of the terms employed – their highly provisional status – and the fact that thought simply cannot manage without them in the work of deconstruction. By this graphic means, much akin to the anomalous spelling of *differance*, concepts are perpetually shaken and dislodged.

Thus far, then, Derrida and Heidegger seem to pursue very similar deconstructive ends. Their difference opens up at the point where Heidegger locates the source and ground of authentic thought: that is, in the moment of Being or plenitude which precedes articulate discourse. For Derrida this can only represent another classic case of the familiar metaphysical hankering after truth and origins. Heidegger's entire hermeneutic is founded on a notion of truth as self-presence which ultimately seeks to efface, or claims to precede, the play of signification. Where Nietzsche looked back beyond Socrates to a diverse and shifting prehistory of thought, Heidegger looks to a source of authentic truth in the unitary ground of Being. His 'destruction' of metaphysics is intended not, like Derrida's, to release a multiplicity of meaning but to call meaning back to its proper, self-identical source. Heidegger thus stands as Derrida's nearest tactical ally and yet – by this crucial divergence – as his major modern antagonist.

The struggle is enacted most visibly in their respective readings of Nietzsche. Heidegger's treatment is itself confined, as Derrida sees it, to 'a hermeneutic space of the question of truth (of Being)'. It partakes of the same logocentric myth – the craving for origins, truth and presence – which Derrida is everywhere at pains to uncover. Here it is a question, he argues, of noting the uncanny disruptions and obliquities of *style* which wrench Heidegger's project away from its professed aim. His reading irresistibly yields 'to a violent yet almost internal necessity and, although not actually undone, . . . is forced to open onto still another reading which for its part refuses to be contained there' (Derrida 1979, p. 115). The unsettling power of Nietzsche's text is such as to place it beyond reach of a philosophy aimed, like Heidegger's, towards truth and the ultimate presence of meaning. Hence the style of outlandish virtuosity – the ruses of metaphor and image – which Derrida by contrast brings to his reading of Nietzsche. Interpretation is no longer turned back in a deluded quest for origins and truth. Rather, it assumes the vertiginous freedom of writing itself: a writing launched by the encounter with a text which itself acknowledges no limit to the free play of meaning.

Nietzsche's umbrella

This ludic or playful dimension is very much a part of Derrida's refusal to subjugate 'writing' to 'philosophy', or style to the kind of repressive regime that treats figurative language as a blemish on the surface of logical thought. Pushed to an extreme, this means suspending all question as to Nietzsche's likely or intended import, and accepting that his texts exist in a realm of open potential, beyond any hope of assured 'hermeneutic' recovery. Derrida treads the giddy brink of absurdity in the pages he devotes to a marginal jotting in Nietzsche's notebooks: 'I have forgotten my umbrella.' He makes ingenious play with the possible 'meanings' of this fragment, only to conclude – again with Heidegger and the 'hermeneuts' in view – that its context is irretrievable and its meaning therefore a total enigma. Suggestions of a Freudian reading are briefly entertained, then dismissed as betraying that same inveterate itch to make sense – to discover some hidden but 'true' significance – which besets the hermeneutic enterprise. The sentence, Derrida concludes, is neither more nor less 'significant' than any other passage of Nietzsche's writing. Because this text, like any other, is 'structurally liberated' from intentions or living speech, it might always be the case 'that it means nothing, or that it has no decidable meaning . . . the hermeneut cannot but be provoked and disconcerted by its play' (ibid., pp. 131–2).

Derrida thus turns the tables most effectively on Heidegger's reading of Nietzsche as the 'last of the metaphysicians'. On Derrida's account it is Heidegger who uses the traditional sanctions of truth and authenticity to recapture the Nietzschean text for his hermeneutic purposes. Against this philosophy Derrida deploys every possible means of liberating Nietzsche's stylistic energies, allowing his text to 'disseminate' sense beyond all the bounds of conceptual closure. This strategy is often wildly at odds with Nietzsche's manifest meaning. Thus Derrida draws some strange metaphorical connections between Nietzsche's image of *Woman* ('her seductive distance, her captivating inaccessibility, the ever-veiled promise of her provocative transcendence') and *writing* as the non-truth of philosophy, the dissolver of concepts and categorical distinctions (ibid., p. 89). Remembering Nietzsche's notorious misogynist streak ('You are visiting a woman? Don't forget to take your whip'), feminists will doubtless find this as baffling as the average philosopher, faced with Derrida's style of argumentation.

But this is to misunderstand the 'question of the woman' as Derrida half-playfully expounds it from the hints and indirections of Nietzsche's text. He goes on to admonish Heidegger for having silently subsumed 'the sexual question' under the 'more general question of truth'. Hermeneutics is supposedly riven, or wrenched from its quest for truth, by a language of erotic suggestion and teasing *differance* which breaks down its claims to interpretative mastery. Heidegger's reading merely 'idles offshore' in so far as it ignores the disruptive influence of woman in Nietzsche's proliferating chains of metaphor. Derrida can quote very much to the point from a text like *Ecce Homo*, which indeed seems to equate the multiplicity of styles in Nietzsche's writing with his intimate knowledge of women ('perhaps I am the first psychologist of the eternally feminine'). His point, however, is not to document the character of Nietzsche's erotic sensibility but to trace those *textual* feints and suggestions that elude any normative logic of sense. Of course there is nothing self-evident about Derrida's curious equation between woman, sexuality and the swerve from logic into figurative language. What he is out to convey is the effect of a reading which 'perversely' cuts across the normal conventions of relevance and hermeneutic tact.

In Barthes's later writing (notably *A Lover's Discourse*, trans. 1979) there is a similar desire to sexualize language, to yield as it were to the seductive repertoire of images and figures where reason loses its mastery. This is very much in line with Barthes's growing scepticism about the use and attractiveness of structuralist thought when applied with too much methodological rigour. His eroticized 'theory' of the text is a constant nimble evasion of any paternal law which might threaten the pleasures – albeit the highly intellectualized pleasures – of reading. Barthes achieves this effect by a glancing impressionistic way with ideas which nowhere allows them to settle into method or concept. It is no coincidence that Nietzsche provides so many of the starting-points and texts for meditation in *A Lover's Discourse*. Nietzsche's dissolution of categorical language is for Barthes the very image of erotic desire and abandonment.

Derrida likewise deploys an eroticized reading of Nietzsche to unfix and disconcert the hermeneutic project. The 'question of the woman' in Nietzsche 'suspends the decidable opposition of true and non-true . . . whereupon the question of style is immediately unloosed as a question of writing' (Derrida 1979, p. 57). Where Barthes rests content with a wayward and glancing approach to the text, Derrida is impelled to engage its metaphors in a far more strenuous way, responding to the Nietzschean challenge with a strange but rigorously *argued* reading. The scholarly 'problem' of Nietzsche's style is shown to open up into the larger question of how philosophy has so long managed to repress or forget its own status as *writing*. Nietzsche is not 'the last metaphysician' but – as Derrida reads him – the first knowingly to unwrite or deconstruct the history of metaphysics. Along with his compatriot and near-contemporary Karl Marx, he stands among the great demythologizing figures of modern thought. Between them Marx and Nietzsche stake out the main possibilities and rival claims of post-structuralist criticism.

5
Between Marx and Nietzsche: the politics of deconstruction

An interview with Derrida, published in the volume *Positions* (1981), raises the question of political commitment and the link – if any – between Marxism and deconstruction. The interviewers, Jean-Louis Houdebine and Guy Scarpetta, were both speaking for the brand of *Marxisant* textual semiotics associated with the Parisian journal *Tel Quel*. Their questioning took an aggressive line, attempting to pin Derrida down on the issue of whether his 'methods' were allied – or implicitly opposed – to the Marxist analysis of language and ideology. Derrida's response was to argue, in effect, that the texts of Marx and Lenin have yet to be *read* in a rigorous fashion which could draw out their modes of rhetorical and figurative working. They cannot simply be interpreted, he argues, according to a preconceived method which would 'seek out a finished signified beneath a textual surface'. Deconstruction would have to emphasize what Derrida calls the 'heterogeneity' of the Marxist text, the ways in which it breaks with idealist tradition (notably Hegel) while yet showing signs of being governed, at a deeper level, by various metaphysical themes.

Houdebine and Scarpetta tried to nudge the dialogue towards some sort of tactical alliance, perhaps between 'contradiction' (as the mainspring of Marxist dialectic) and Derrida's thematics of *differance*. His replies go to show how radically incompatible are the claims of a self-styled materialist 'science of the text' and those of a deconstruction which sees no prospect of any such total break with ideology. For Derrida, the language of dialectical materialism is shot through with *metaphors* disguised as *concepts*, themes that carry along with them a whole unrecognized baggage of presuppositions. It must henceforth be a question, Derrida says, of taking that language and investigating 'all the sediments deposited [in it] by the history of metaphysics' (see Derrida 1981, pp. 39–91).

This encounter, though brief and inconclusive, points to a major topic of contention in and around the development of Derrida's ideas. Is deconstruction merely – as some of its opponents claim – a newfangled form of textual mystification, helping to keep history and politics at bay? Is it 'undialectical' in its concern with themes of presence and *differance* which persist down the ages and bear no mark of socio-economic change? What is the relation, in short, between Derridean deconstruction and those varieties of Marxist literary theory which have emerged in the wake of structuralism? An approach to these questions can best be made by tracing the two great rival influences on post-structuralist thinking, those of Marx himself and his compatriot Friedrich Nietzsche.

Deconstruction in the Nietzschean mode has produced a discourse of extreme sceptical rigour and rhetorical self-consciousness. The Marxist critique has been equally powerful, on the one hand adopting certain structuralist ideas in developing its own theoretical basis, while on the other rejecting what are seen as elements recalcitrant to Marxist thought. Between these two main trends of post-structuralist theory there has emerged a complex antagonism which brings out the radical *differance* of deconstruction.

Derrida on Hegel

Derrida's virtual silence in regard to Marx can only be construed as a prolonged postponement, a refusal as yet to engage Marxist thought on its own textual ground. Derrida can devote a whole chapter to Hegel (in *Writing and Difference*) without so much as mentioning the Marxist critique and materialist inversion of Hegelian thought. His reading seeks to isolate the point

in Hegel's philosophy where history and consciousness, so far
from uniting in a plenitude of intelligible meaning, find themselves subject to a dislocating movement beyond all grasp of
dialectic. Hegelian logic suffers a rhetorical swerve from purpose which betrays it into self-contradiction through a surplus
of unmanageable meaning. The 'restricted economy' of Hegel's
system is displaced and invaded by a 'general economy' which
Derrida equates with the effects of writing or textuality. Concepts are unfixed from their 'lawful' philosophic place, subjected to a violent 'mutation of meaning' and turned back
against the sovereignty of reason. 'Since no logic governs,
henceforth, the meaning of interpretation, because logic is an
interpretation, Hegel's own interpretation can be reinterpreted
– against him' (Derrida 1978, p. 260). In typical Derridean
fashion, the essay approaches Hegel not directly but via another
reading – that of Georges Bataille – whose perceptions and
blind-spots are a further pretext for deconstructive treatment.
Hegel's argument is cunningly enmeshed in a web of intertextual significations which place it far beyond any single, authoritative logic.

Elsewhere in *Writing and Difference* Derrida broaches the
relation between text and politics, suggesting briefly that deconstruction offers 'the premises for a non-Marxist reading of
philosophy as ideology'. Certainly his reading of Hegel brings
out the conflict between deconstruction and anything like a
Marxist understanding of textual ideology. Hegelian dialectic
becomes only one chapter in the Western tradition of logocentric discourse pushed up against its limits by the 'general
economy' of writing. There is little sense of its historical rooted-
ness, or indeed of its role as an antagonist-precursor to Marxist
thought. History is reduced to the play of *representations* by which
the mind, on Hegel's account, attempts to take hold of its own
understanding and the stages of historical thought which led up
to it. At the limit-point of conscious reflection, history dissolves
into the figures of rhetoric where all claims to knowledge are
deconstructed. Hegel's dialectic of power and knowledge can be
turned on its head by a reading which fastens on those points
where metaphor disrupts the very logic of his argument. Hegelian history can be read 'from left to right or from right to left, as
a reactionary movement or as a revolutionary movement, or

both at once' (ibid., p. 276). The figural play or 'supplementarity' of writing makes it impossible to subordinate meaning to a preconceived system of explanation. The conceptual 'totality' is always undone by the ruses of signification, those 'slidings and differences of discourse' that deconstruction is at pains to uncover.

As we have seen, it was Nietzsche who first brought such a sceptical critique to bear on the systematic edifice of Hegelian philosophy. For Nietzsche, as for Derrida, the project of absolute knowledge was deluded at source by its forgetfulness of how *language* creates and capriciously misleads the processes of thought. Nietzsche saw nothing but blindness and multiplied error in the various attempts to arrive at truth through logic or abstract reason. Philosophy had based itself unwittingly on a series of buried metaphors none the less potent and beguiling for their common and commonsense usage. Nietzsche carries out what amounts to a full-scale programme of deconstruction, attacking every last vestige of philosophic truth and certainty. The fundamental 'laws' of Aristotelian logic are held to be expressions of our present *inability* to think beyond them, rather than possessing an absolute validity. Logic is the product of a will to understand which selectively arranges the habits of thought so as to make some sense of immediate experience. Concepts are formed on the groundless supposition that our *knowledge* of objects in the world comes directly from our *experience* of what it is to perceive them. The link between empirical self-evidence and conceptual truth is, according to Nietzsche, a species of metaphorical displacement, raising the contingent into the necessary by a constant (though unrecognized) leverage of tropes.

Nietzsche therefore stands as a precursor to that line of post-structuralist thought which questions the very concepts of method and 'structure' in the name of a demystifying rhetoric. As Derrida makes clear in his essay on Hegel, this questioning extends to the field of historical knowledge, in so far as such knowledge claims a basis in absolute reason. The 'meaning of history' and the 'history of meaning' are bound up together in that quest for self-authenticating truth that is endemic to Western thought. Hegel's belief in the 'ontological unity of method and historicity' is the point at which Derrida locates the repeated hankering for origins and self-presence. Hegel treats history and consciousness as converging towards a stage of maximum lucidity and consummate understanding. Derrida – like Nietzsche before him – sets out to deconstruct this idealized knowledge and the concepts of method which belong to it.

In so doing, he throws down an outright challenge to the powers of historical explanation. This might seem merely another, more sophisticated version of the quarrel between 'synchronic' and 'diachronic' modes of thought which marked the early stages of structuralist debate. Lévi-Strauss presented the issues most clearly in his essay 'History and Dialectic' (in Lévi-Strauss 1966). This took the form of a reply to those (including Sartre) who had condemned structuralism as an abstract methodology and a flight from the realities of history and lived experience. Such objections were merely, in Lévi-Strauss's view, a product of the outworn illusion that attached historical significance to meanings secreted by the individual mind in the process of self-projection. History was rather to be seen as a series of shifting configurative patterns, the 'meaning' of which becomes increasingly opaque with the passage of time. 'Events which are significant for one code are no longer so for another'; what meaning they possess is entirely dependent on how they strike a contemporary. Historical understanding is only possible in so far as it adopts a synchronic standpoint, 'classes of dates each furnishing an autonomous system of reference'. Sartre's idea of 'totalization' – of history unfolding its significance through a sweep of interpretative hindsight – is dismissed by Lévi-Strauss as a wishful belief in the wholeness and continuity of human experience. This belief attaches a 'spurious intelligibility' to events that have only a shifting and provisional significance. To 'socialize the Cogito' in Sartre's fashion is to fall into the twin Hegelian traps of 'individualism and empiricism'.

Marxism, structuralism and deconstruction

This quarrel was taken up by critics like Frederic Jameson, Marxists of a broadly structuralist persuasion who felt that the claims of synchronic thought must somehow be reconciled with those of historical understanding. Jameson agrees with Lévi-

Strauss in so far as he treats interpretation as a process of perpetual 'transcoding', a rhetorical activity conscious of its own operations and never coming to rest in a single, determinate 'truth'. Such a method would result, Jameson argues, in a new-found openness of critical discourse and a way of transcending those hateful contraries, 'form' and 'content'. Where his argument distinctly lacks force is in the claim that this open plurality of codes would effectively involve both critic and literary work in a process of deeper *historical* engagement. After so much tight-knit argumentation, Jameson's phraseology here is revealingly loose and metaphorical. By showing the variety of codes at work on both sides of every interpretative act, structuralism promises 'to reopen text and analytic process alike to all the winds of history' (Jameson 1971, p. 216).

Jameson's confident *rapprochement* between rhetoric and Marxist dialectic can only seem premature in the light of subsequent developments. Others, like Terry Eagleton, have recognized more clearly that an open-ended free play of rhetorical transcoding – with the ideal of an infinitely 'plural' text – is resistant to the purposes of Marxist criticism. Jameson pins his theory to a faith that *method* can retain some absolute validity even when history and meaning have been reduced to a constantly shifting interplay of tropes. He sides, in other words, with that element in Lévi-Strauss's thinking which seeks to preserve 'structure' as a mode of intelligibility immune to the assaults of sceptical doubt.

It is precisely this 'version' of structuralism that Derrida so deftly dismantles in the texts of Saussure and Lévi-Strauss. His object is not to deny or invalidate the structuralist project but to show how its deepest implications lead on to a questioning of method more extreme and unsettling than these thinkers wish to admit. The very notion of 'structure' is shown to be a metaphor dependent, at the limit, on a willed forgetting of its own rhetorical status. Two of Derrida's most powerful essays – 'Force and Signification' and 'Structure, Sign and Play' – are devoted to precisely this end of bringing out the radical metaphoricity of 'structure' as a term and an operative concept. Otherwise, he argues, one remains for ever trapped in the circular logic of a discourse which ceaselessly confirms its own truth. 'Structure' is ultimately a reflex image of the visual or spatial metaphors to which Western thought has so often resorted in its quest for understanding.

To think without the aid of such figurative props may well be beyond the powers of mind. To accept them, on the other hand, without deconstructing their effects is to risk 'being interested in the figure itself to the detriment of the play going on within it metaphorically' (Derrida 1978, p. 16). Derrida is following Nietzsche's critique of the delusions engendered by moving metaphorically from image to concept without subjecting that movement to a full rhetorical scrutiny. The great virtue of structuralism, on Derrida's account, is that it poses this necessity in the most urgent terms: 'Does the fact that language can determine things only by spatializing them suffice to explain that, in return, language must spatialize itself as soon as it designates and reflects upon itself?' (ibid.). Constantly to raise such questions about its own methods and validity is for Derrida the only means by which structuralism can avoid the nemesis of 'structure'.

As I have argued, it is difficult to square deconstruction in this radical, Nietzschean guise with any workable Marxist account of text and ideology. Such attempted fusions in the name of a Marxian post-structuralist theory are fated, for reasons I shall now pursue, to an endlessly proliferating discourse of abstraction. To deconstruct a text in Nietzschean-Derridean terms is to arrive at a limit-point or deadlocked *aporia* of meaning which offers no hold for Marxist-historical understanding. The textual 'ideology' uncovered by Derrida's readings is a kind of aboriginal swerve into metaphor and figurative detour which language embraces through an error of thought unaccountable in Marxist terms.

Eagleton's one brief reference to Nietzsche in *Criticism and Ideology* (1976) manifests the unease a Marxist must feel in the face of such thoroughgoing scepticism. His immediate target is the Parisian journal *Tel Quel*'s brand of 'libertarian' textual theory, which equates radical politics with the free play of an infinitely pluralized meaning. This attitude typically inverts itself (on Eagleton's reading) 'into a mirror-image of bourgeois social relations'. To invest all meaning in the freedom from a single, authoritative meaning – invoking it only to deny – is an impotent gesture of defiance. But Eagleton's real quarry here is

Nietzsche and the Nietzschean challenge to a Marxist interpretative theory. There are, he remarks, other kinds of radical
break with tradition

> which are not fixated in the moment of release which follows
> on the dethronement of the ultimate donor of meaning –
> which accept that if God is dead there is no need to resurrect
> Nietzsche, since their reference-point is the 'taken-for-
> granted' post-atheism of Marx rather than the 'always-to-be-
> validated' post-atheism of his compatriot.   (Eagleton 1976,
> p. 43)

Nietzschean scepticism becomes here a kind of infantile dis-
order, shown up for what it is by the certified maturity of
Marxist-historical thought. Deconstruction might be seen in
the same negative terms: a discourse fixated upon the 'transcendental signified' of logocentric thought, self-locked (like
Nietzsche) in the toils of endless demystification.

But on what ground precisely does Eagleton rest this higher
dialectical knowledge? On the precondition, as he states it
(following Althusser), that criticism must 'break with its ideological prehistory, situating itself outside the space of the text on
the alternative terrain of scientific knowledge' (ibid., p. 43). The
metaphors here are manifestly visual and spatial. They cry out
to be deconstructed, not merely in a spirit of perverse oneupmanship, but in order to follow through their implications for
Marxist epistemology. Eagleton's imagery of textual 'space'
and scientific 'terrain' derives from a refined but omnipresent
version of the base/superstructure metaphor. Theory (or a
putative 'science of the text') is seen as placing itself outside and
above the domain of lived ideology. The literary text stands
midway between them, a rich but confused source of knowledge, more 'immediate' than theory in its access to experience
but so representing and *working* that experience as to make it
accessible (visible) to theory. Such is the basis for Eagleton's
'science of the text': 'In yielding up to criticism the ideologically
determined conventionality of its modes of constructing sense,
the text at the same time obliquely illuminates the relation of
that ideology to real history' (ibid., p. 101). The argument here
is entirely in the charge of its sustaining metaphors, the process
envisaged as a vertical ascent to a plane of science and lucidity

from the 'vivid but loose contingencies' of lived experience. The 'oblique illumination' offered by the literary text is oblique in so far as it occupies that relatively dense middle region; 'illuminating' in the measure that it yields itself up to knowledge. The metaphors of light and darkness co-operate with those of hierarchical structure to produce a perfect *image* – or visual analogon – of the textual science that Eagleton has in mind.

Derrida's essay 'The White Mythology' (1974b) has much to say about the figural implications of light and darkness as they permeate the texts of Western philosophy. Reason, the natural light of intelligence, is typically opposed to the opaque materiality not only of inanimate nature but of writing as an alien and obtrusive medium. This is, of course, the root strategy of logocentric discourse which Derrida turns back against itself by forcing its logic to the point of implicit reversal. That consciousness can be present to itself in the pure light of reason, delivered from the snares of opaque textuality, is a recurrent dream of Western thought. It is deeply embedded in the Marxist theory of text, ideology and representation, even where that theory is meticulously purged of crude deterministic thinking. The 'science' proposed by Eagleton, Pierre Macherey and other Althusserian Marxists cannot in the end break loose from the visual and spatial metaphors that determine its logic. Texts are treated as a more or less 'dense', 'opaque' or 'obliquely' translucent writing placed between the raw stuff of lived experience and the penetrating light of knowledge. The etymological link between 'theory' and 'seeing' (Greek *thea* = spectacle) becomes a forgotten or sublimated metaphor underlying the certitudes of science.

The figurative texture of Eagleton's language is most in evidence where his theory comes up against the problems of defining 'representation' in a materialist but non-reductive sense. The text 'represents' ideology by revealing 'in peculiarly intense, compacted and coherent form the categories from which those representations are produced' (Eagleton 1976, p. 101). The argument here is borne up by a circular exchange of metaphorical values attaching to the spatial and visual connotations of the language employed. A sense of rigour and explanatory power is conveyed by the abstract term 'categories', which yet remains contextually ill defined. Its want of specificity is made up for rhetorically by the hints of a concrete, vivid directness in words like 'intense' and 'compacted'. The visual-projective metaphors of 'form' and 'representation' complete the work of *conceptualizing* this tight-knit cluster of images. What the literary text reveals is the condition of its own intelligibility as *viewed* from precisely this figurative standpoint.

Eagleton does indeed qualify his position, but in equally symptomatic language:

> 'Reveals' is perhaps a misleading term here, for not every text displays its ideological categories on its surface: the visibility of those categories depends on the text's precise modes of working them, as well as on the nature of the categories themselves.   (ibid., p. 85)

The metaphors here are even more insistent. Ideology is 'displayed' by the text, at whatever depth from its specular surface, through a mode of more or less 'visible' working produced by those same abstract 'categories'. Eagleton's elaborate argumentation cannot conceal its dependence on these basic and proliferating figures of thought. It is ironic that he should elsewhere criticize Althusser and Macherey for their retreat into a 'nebulously figurative' discourse which gives their arguments a 'merely rhetorical quality'. For all his alertness to this slippage into metaphor, Eagleton exhibits the same liability, most often indeed when he is expounding a new Marxist 'science' which will mark the break with such ideological discourse. The Marxist model of representation, however refined in theory, is caught up in a rhetoric of tropes and images that entirely controls its logic.

Nietzsche *contra* Marx?

This puts a very different slant on Eagleton's summary contrast between Marx and Nietzsche. The 'taken-for-granted' basis of historical materialism is challenged in its subtlest formulations by the 'always-to-be-validated' Nietzschean critique. Deconstruction is inimical to Marxist thought at the point where it questions the validity of *any* science or method set up in rigid separation from the play of textual meaning. Jameson and Eagleton represent the opposite faces of a common dilemma. Jameson assimilates history and meaning to an open-ended free play where, as we have seen, historical method becomes little more than an optional gesture of commitment. Eagleton rejects this pluralist outlook and argues resourcefully for a knowledge of the text which would measure its distance from the effects of rhetorical duplicity and error. But for criticism to step outside the textual domain and achieve such knowledge *in other than figurative terms* is a task beyond its reach. The end-point of deconstructive thought, as Derrida insists, is to recognize that there is no end to the interrogative play between text and text. Deconstruction can never have the final word because its insights are inevitably couched in a rhetoric which itself lies open to further deconstructive reading. Criticism can only be deluded in its claim to operate (as Eagleton puts it) 'outside the space of the text' on a plane of scientific knowledge. There is no metalanguage.

Althusserian Marxism is a form of deconstruction, but one that seeks to halt the process at a point where science can extract the hidden message of ideology. This movement of arrest in the name of some determining system or structure is the strategy that Derrida dismantles in his essay 'Force and Signification'. It involves a crucial blindness to elements of rhetoric which – as in Eagleton's case – can be read deconstructively to bring out their figural evasions. Marxist criticism invites such a reading when it assumes a post-structuralist theoretical standpoint. Jameson and Eagleton share this assumption in so far as they treat the text as a rhetorical construct which 'works' ideology into new, problematic formations accessible to scientific reading. They accept, that is, the structuralist divorce between text and reality, regarding 'the real' as an *effect* produced by certain culturally privileged codes of representation. With Jameson, indeed, it is hard to distinguish the Marxist case for a 'productive' textuality from the Barthesian ecstasy of liberated meaning. Eagleton avoids this total abandonment to rhetoric, but only by constraining his text to ignore what would otherwise call its method into question. His metaphors hypostatize an image of the relation between text, ideology and science which in turn depends upon figurative detours conspicuously open to deconstructive reading.

Once criticism enters the labyrinth of deconstruction, it is committed to a sceptical epistemology that leads back to

Nietzsche, rather than Marx, as the end-point of its quest for method. Nietzschean 'method' is no more perhaps than a lesson in perpetual self-defeat, but a lesson more rigorous and searching than the compromise assurances of post-structuralist Marxism. Pierre Macherey exhibits the same crucial blind-spot in his efforts to preserve the 'scientific' status of criticism against the various beguilements and obfuscating rhetoric of the text. 'The real, as it is formulated in the discourse of the work, is always arbitrary because it depends entirely on the unfolding of this discourse' (Macherey 1978, p. 37). Deconstructionist readings take the same line of argument to show how narrative discourse typically produces a kind of paradoxical logic which undercuts its own referential or realist pretensions. Macherey goes on to insist that 'the themes immediately extracted from *literary* works can have no initial value as concepts' (ibid., p. 21). This would seem to accord with Nietzsche's sceptical injunction against passing too easily from image to concept. But Macherey still thinks of critical 'science' as a discourse which can so completely free itself from textual constraints as to see right through to the underlying conflicts of literary ideology. (For a fuller account and critique of Macherey's thinking, see Belsey 1980.) He takes it as axiomatic that criticism can break with the whole delusive rhetoric of textual representation. What this axiom suppresses is the knowledge that criticism also constructs itself as a discourse of tropes and analogies all the more beguiling for its scientific claims.

Foucault and Said: the rhetoric of power

This conflict of interpretations is at the heart of current post-structuralist debate. Michel Foucault has gone furthest toward spelling out the implications of Nietzschean thought for the project of Marxist and historical-interpretative method. In the following passage he describes the rift between these two competing orders of knowledge:

> In appearance, or rather, according to the mask it bears, historical consciousness is neutral, devoid of passions, and committed solely to truth. But if it examines itself and if, more generally, it interrogates the various forms of scientific consciousness in its history, it finds that all these forms

and transformations are aspects of the will to knowledge: instinct, passion, the inquisitor's devotion, cruel subtlety, and
malice.   (Foucault 1977, p. 162)

Nietzsche's challenge to Marx (an issue Foucault strategically
skirts) goes along with this radically textual or figurative mode
of understanding the ruses of history. It disrupts all those
metaphors of access-to-truth by which 'scientific' method sustains its immunity from question. Foucault, like Nietzsche,
adopts what he calls a 'dissociating view' of historical meaning,
one that sets out to shatter 'the unity of man's being through
which it was thought he could extend his sovereignty to the
events of his past' (ibid., p. 154).

Foucault's Nietzschean rhetoric amounts to an activist rewriting of Derrida's text on Hegel. It sets out to create a
maximum disturbance in the charmed circle of exchange where
history, consciousness and meaning coincide in the mastery of
knowledge. Foucault's critique would equally apply to a Marxist 'science' convinced of its power to escape the figurality of
language and achieve a perspective atop all the conflicts of
meaning. It is no longer, he argues, 'a question of judging the
past in the name of a truth which only we can possess in the
present'. History writing on Nietzschean terms involves a sur-
render of the privileged claim to knowledge once entertained by
the sovereign consciousness. It becomes a question, in
Foucault's words, of 'risking the destruction of the subject who
seeks knowledge in the endless deployment of the will to knowledge' (ibid., p. 164). Such is the effect of applying a Nietzschean
or deconstructive rhetoric of tropes to the self-possessed categories of Marxist-structuralist thought.

What might come of this postponed encounter between
Marxist and Nietzschean theories of the text? Jeffrey Mehlman's *Revolution and Repetition* (1979) gives a brief but trenchant
example of how deconstruction can press upon the strategies
of Marxist discourse and draw out its textual aberrations.
Mehlman shrewdly latches his argument to 'The Eighteenth
Brumaire of Louis Bonaparte', one of Marx's most eccentric
and anomalous texts (Marx 1968). The republic of the Nephew
is seen as an absurdity defeating all the laws of dialectic, a
clownish repetition of historical events which utterly disrupts

the Marxist categories. History repeats itself as farce; reason is confronted with images of a prodigal stupidity which numb its powers. Mehlman shows how this bafflement infects the very texture of Marx's prose, erupting into metaphors and fantastic processions of senseless but colourful detail. Bonapartism is the 'scandal' of Marxian thought, the 'systematic dispersion' (as Mehlman reads it) of any theory attempting to link historical events with a logic of *representation*. The sheer descriptive relish of Marx's text – its listing of absurd, unassimilable detail – works perversely to undermine dialectical reason. *Napoléon le Petit* becomes not merely a parody of the Uncle but the instance of a 'generalised parasitism' gnawing at the bases of Marxist-historical thought. 'Revolution' as the term of dialectic gives way to a grotesque 'repetition' voiding the significance of history.

Foucault has described these effects of textual repetition in his essay on Gilles Deleuze. What they bring into play is an undifferentiated, non-categorical surplus of meaning which mocks and destroys the putative laws of thought. Dialectics depend upon categories that 'organise the play of affirmations and negations, establish the legitimacy of representation, and guarantee the objectivity and operation of concepts' (Foucault 1977, p. 186). Repetition, on the other hand, breaks down all those explanatory systems of history and knowledge which depend upon a logic of identity and non-contradiction. It takes hold (as in Mehlman's reading of Marx) where 'the barely-launched mediation falls back on itself . . . when it constantly returns to the same position, instead of distributing oppositions within a system of finite elements' (ibid.). Such irruptions of uncontrolled meaning are the points at which textuality asserts itself against any form of absolute methodical constraint.

This is not to condemn critical theory, as some would suppose, to an endless play of self-occupied textual abstraction. Rather it is to recognize, with Foucault, that texts and interpretative strategies compete for domination in a field staked out by no single order of validating method. Foucault follows Nietzsche in deconstructing those systems of thought which mask their incessant will to power behind a semblance of objective knowledge. His analysis of these various 'discursive practices' constantly points to their being involved in a politics none the less real for its inextricably textual character. Edward Said, in his book *Orientalism* (1978), has offered a very practical example of how deconstruction can engage cultural history on its own textual ground and contest its claims to objectivity. The image of 'the Orient' constructed by generations of scholars, poets and historians is shown to be governed by an ethnocentric discourse secure in the power of its superior wisdom. Occidental reason is confirmed point for point in its mythography of oriental laziness, guile and 'exotic' irrationalism. To combat this discourse by exposing its ruses of metaphor is not to set up as a 'science' unmasking the confusions of ideology. It is an act of challenge which situates itself on rhetorical ground the better to meet and turn back the claims of a spurious objectivity.

Said has argued the case for this approach in his recent essay 'The Text, the World, the Critic' (1979). Texts are irreducibly 'worldly' in the sense that they take on a circumstantial setting and lead a varied afterlife of meanings and *uses* which place them squarely in the public domain. Discourse is incapable of sustaining itself in what Said calls 'a hermetic, Alexandrian textual universe, having no connection with actuality'. Texts are in and of the world because they lend themselves to strategies of reading whose intent is always part of a struggle for interpretative power. It is a similar impulse – according to Said – that induces the novelist to weave into his fiction details of circumstance and context that insist on its narrative veracity. Fiction has always involved this sense of an 'unwillingness to cede control over the text . . . to release it from the discursive obligations of human presence' (Said 1979, p. 177). The control may indeed be illusory, a wishful projection of authorial power; but it reflects an awareness that texts exist from the outset as ground to be competed for by various strategies of self-promoting knowledge.

It is surely no coincidence that one of Said's examples is the same text of Marx ('The Eighteenth Brumaire') that Mehlman singles out for deconstructive treatment. Said's observations are similar up to a point. He notes the disruptive effects of 'repetition', the way in which the text 'inserts' Louis Bonaparte into a sequence of outrageous roles and correspondences which elude any rational account. Said, however, reaches a conclusion rather different from Mehlman's, and one that supports the hrust of his argument for understanding texts as bearers of a worldly', practical meaning. Mehlman interprets 'The Eight-eenth Brumaire' as a kind of rhetorical affront to history, a monstrous and proliferating discourse which takes on its own absurd narrative power. Said sees all this, but is struck more forcibly by the strange *correspondence* between this egregious text and the order of historical events. Like the novelist – but to an even higher pitch of obsession – Marx fills in every circumstan-cial detail to underline the Nephew's role as 'farcical repetition' of the Uncle. The text's sheer density of documentation is oddly reinforced by a pattern of narrative links that lends it a kind of perverse authenticating logic. Textual strategies become, para-doxically, a means of explaining the absurd contingencies of historical happening. That this explanation issues in parodic or 'repetitive' form is precisely a measure of its power to convince.

What really challenges understanding, in Said's view, is the question of how a text, 'by being a text, by insisting upon and employing all the devices of textuality, preeminent among them *repetition*, historicizes and problematizes all the fugitive signi-ficance which has chosen Louis Bonaparte as its representative' (ibid., p. 178). There is no room here for that too simple contrast between 'the world' and 'the text' which Said regards as a falsification of deconstructive thought. His approach to these problems is persuasive in its power to combine a rigorous textual awareness with a practical involvement in the politics of reading. It is not, like so much post-Althusserian Marxist theory, locked in the problems of a discourse fixated upon its own formulations and unable to recognize their figurative nature. Only by following through the logic of deconstruction, rather than meeting its challenge halfway, can thought escape this imprisonment by the metaphors of its own frozen discourse. Nietzsche remains at the last a disturbing threat to the 'taken-for-granted' rhetoric of Marxist theory.

6

The American connection

For the past ten years or so Derrida has been dividing his time between Paris and America, mainly through his visiting professorships at Yale and Johns Hopkins universities. His following among American critics has grown apace, and it is now safe to say that he exerts a greater influence on them than any of his fellow French post-structuralists. This is evident from the sheer volume of critical writing that nowadays bears the deconstructionist imprint, whether openly acknowledged or (more often) betrayed by certain characteristic turns of argument or phrase. Derrida himself has entered with alacrity into the various discussions sparked off by his writing. To disciples and opponents alike he has responded with a number of prolix and mind-wrenching texts designed for translation and wittily exploiting the inherent ambiguities of the medium. In some of these essays the playful inclination – already well developed in his writing on Nietzsche – seems to outrun any content of serious argument. But one needs to exercise a good deal of caution when applying such conventional measures of worth to texts that explicitly put them in question. Perhaps the most radical effect of Derrida's writing has been to transform the very notion of what counts as 'serious' critical thought.

Individual critics have responded very differently to Derrida's example, so that even to speak of a deconstructionist 'movement' is already to blur some vital distinctions of emphasis and style. In Chapter 5 I pointed to one such divergence, the debate that has lately sprung up between the purist deconstructors and those (like Edward Said) who wish to restore the text to a 'worldly' or political dimension of meaning. In broadly institutional terms, Yale and Johns Hopkins have done most to disseminate Derridean theory in its resolutely textual – and largely apolitical – form. The Marxist or activist challenge has hitherto come from outside, though now, with Frederic Jameson teaching at Yale, the debate is being pressed nearer home. But even within the group of critics most closely identified with Derrida's thinking – Geoffrey Hartman, Paul de Man and J. Hillis Miller – differences emerge which suggest a certain ambivalence about the aims and priorities of deconstruction. This ambivalence is also more marked in the texts Derrida has produced at the bidding (or provocation) of his American colleagues.

A passage from *Of Grammatology* may help to focus the difference at issue here. Deconstruction, Derrida writes,

> always in a certain way falls prey to its own work. This is what the person who has begun the same work in another area of the same habitation does not fail to point out with zeal. No exercise is more widespread today and one should be able to formalize its rules.   (Derrida 1977a, p. 24)

The 'exercise' is very much more widespread now than when Derrida wrote these words. The zeal for deconstruction has not, on the other hand, always gone along with the kind of argumentative rigour Derrida calls for here. Indeed, its appeal for some critics rests very largely on the promise of an open-ended free play of style and speculative thought, untrammelled by 'rules' of any kind. This response has characterized much of what passes for American deconstructionist criticism, at least in its more publicized varieties. With the notable exception of Paul de Man – whose texts display an early-Derridean incisiveness and rigour – the Yale critics have mostly opted for deconstruction on its dizzy, exuberant side. This is not to say that the two can be firmly distinguished, or that one side merits less 'serious' attention than the other. It points, rather, to a choice between rigour and freedom to which Derrida's texts have themselves responded in very different ways.

Deconstruction 'on the wild side': Geoffrey Hartman and J. Hillis Miller

We have seen how deconstruction 'arrived' in America at just the right moment to attract those critics, like Geoffrey Hartman, who had begun to fret under the various constraints of New Critical method. It offered the enticing prospect of a criticism free to explore whatever stylistic possibilities it chose, without observing any strict demarcation between 'creative' and (merely) 'critical' writing. Hartman makes the point most exuberantly in his essay 'The Interpreter: A Self-Analysis' (in Hartman 1975, pp. 3–19). The piece begins with a forthright confession: 'I have a superiority complex vis-à-vis other critics, and an inferiority complex vis-à-vis art.' He then proceeds to dismantle both these burdensome conditions by playing them off in a style of paradoxical argument which brings 'the interpreter' out on a level (of inventiveness, cunning, rhetorical power) with the text he interprets. Like Derrida, he argues that origins are delusive, that texts are always 'belated' with regard to the tradition they inhabit, just as critics feel themselves humbly confined to a secondary role of mere explication. For Hartman, the only way out is for the critic to throw off his 'inferiority complex' and enter wholeheartedly – with a Nietz-schean swagger – into the dance of meaning.

> I think that is where we are now. We have entered an era that can challenge even the priority of literary to literary-critical texts. Longinus is studied as seriously as the sublime texts he comments on; Jacques Derrida on Rousseau almost as interestingly as Rousseau.   (ibid., p. 18)

Or, for that matter, Hartman on Derrida on Rousseau . . . the argument is at no pains to conceal its self-interested character. Quite simply, for Hartman, 'writing is living in the secondary, knowing it is the secondary. That is the curse, or the blessing.'

Hartman often taxes the reader's patience with his virtuoso style and his use of interpretative problems as a sounding-board for his own private struggles. All the same, his writing does convey the exhilarating spirit, the glimpse of new horizons, brought about by Derrida's influence. He and Hillis Miller have been the readiest to follow Derrida's ideas to the limit of interpretative freedom. Miller presents his own self-defence in an essay that cunningly deconstructs the oppositional semantics of the words 'host' and 'parasite' ('The Critic as Host', 1977). He traces a mazy route through the twin etymologies, showing how their meanings cross and redouble until both seem to partake of an ambivalent, almost symbiotic relationship where the 'host' (text) is at least as parasitic as the 'parasite' (critic). Miller's etymological procedures and his ploy of strategically reversing a traditional metaphor, are both powerful tactics borrowed from Derrida. They lead to the upshot of his argument: that critics are no more 'parasites' than the texts they interpret, since both inhabit a host-text of pre-existent language which itself parasitically feeds on their host-like willingness to receive it. Such arguments can clearly be put to a great variety of tactical uses. Miller extends his semantic juggling to the question of whether deconstructionist readings are 'parasitic' (as M. H. Abrams had claimed) on normal or main-line historical interpretations. He is able to demonstrate, once again, that the norm not only presupposes but in some sense *contains* whatever deviations it is required to exclude.

Miller puts these ruses to work in a style that emulates, though it doesn't fully match, the rigour of Derrida's arguments. He is ultimately concerned, like Hartman, to justify this new-found interpretative freedom by seeking out twists of figure and meaning that suit his paradoxical purpose. Miller's receptiveness to deconstruction can be traced back to problems raised but only partially answered in his previous criticism. During the sixties and early seventies his thinking was much influenced by a group of critics – the so-called 'Geneva School' – who saw interpretation as an effort to grasp the *states of awareness* embodied in literary texts. Most prominent among them were Jean Starobinski, Jean-Pierre Richard, Georges Poulet and Jean Rousset. Their general approach was set out by Miller in an article ('The Geneva School', 1966) which offered a useful introduction to the group for most English-speaking readers. Poulet and his colleagues thought of criticism 'as beginning and ending in a coincidence of the mind of the critic and the mind of the author'. The aim was always 'to re-create as precisely as possible the exact tone which persists in a given writer throughout all the variety of his work'.

For Miller this clearly represented a welcome break with the doctrines of American formalism. It also provided a promising alternative to the various rival theories – Freudian, Marxist and others – which had not yet succeeded in challenging the pedagogic rule of New Criticism. By rejecting such methods and focusing instead on the forms of *consciousness* evoked by literary texts, the Geneva critics were helping to free interpretation from the dead hand of critical abstraction. Most importantly for Miller, they had no use for the *spatialized* concepts of form and structure which had gained such a hold on American criticism. Literature was not to be reduced to 'an objective structure of meanings residing in the words of a poem or novel'. Neither was it 'the unwitting expression of a writer's unconscious', nor indeed 'a revelation of the latent structures of exchange which integrate a society'. Texts were primarily there to be experienced, their meanings 'brought into the open' through a process of ideally sympathetic re-creation on the critic's part.

This dream of a perfect, unimpeded communion of minds goes deep in Miller's 'pre-deconstructionist' writing, as it does for Hartman and other American critics whose temperamental homeground is Romantic poetry. Romanticism holds out the utopian idea of a merging between mind and object, a state of awareness so finely attuned to experience that all such distinctions drop away and the knower is at one with the known. Wordsworth's poetry was a constant search for these privileged moments or 'spots of time', while Coleridge pursued a similar theme through the toils of idealist metaphysics. The inherent pathos of this attempt – the fact that the mind can never achieve such perfect communion – is often manifest in Hartman's more chastened style. In 'The Interpreter: A Self-Analysis' he recalls how his criticism at first aspired to a direct, 'unmediated' communing with the text; then, as the ideal receded, how he found ambiguous comfort in the speculative byways opened up to thought by its own self-conscious operations (Hartman 1975, pp. 3–19). The pattern for Hartman's confessional narrative is clearly Wordsworth's *Prelude*, where the poet looks back to his moments of illumination with a sense of belatedness and well-nigh unbridgeable distance. For Hartman this is the impasse encountered by all Romantic and post-Romantic thought. The 'unmediated vision' lies beyond reach of language, because

language brings along with it a mediating structure of awareness which can never coincide with its object in a pure, self-
authenticating knowledge. This was the burden of Hartman's
criticism long before he met with its powerful formulation in the
texts of Derrida. All the same, one can see what impact those
texts must have had on a critic already prone to meditate on the
delusiveness of origins, the myth of self-presence and the
mediating agency of language.

There is much the same development visible in Hillis Miller's
shift from a 'criticism of consciousness' to a mode of deconstructionist thought. His faith in the Geneva critics was pinned to
their assumption that mind could be somehow present to mind
in a purely intuitive transfer of meaning and awareness. In his
1966 essay Miller quotes (approvingly) the view of Georges
Poulet that language at its most expressive is a perfectly *transparent* medium, allowing the critic to enter fully into the author's
state of mind. By the time of his *Thomas Hardy: Distance and Desire*
(1970), this position is already coming under strain from
Miller's use of *textual* images in place of those metaphors drawn
from consciousness itself. The critic's mode of entry, Miller
writes,

> is language, a medium within which he already dwells. He
> can insert himself into the text because both he and it are
> already interpenetrated by their common language. The
> means of his interpretation is also language, those words of
> his which even in the most passive act of reading he adds to
> the text as he understands it . . .   (Miller 1970, p. 36)

This passage can perhaps be made to square with the Genevan
ideal of a criticism wholly given up to the interplay of mind with
mind through the perfect transparency of language. But, whatever his intentions, Miller's terminology now insists on the
endlessly *textual* nature of all understanding, the way in which
meanings are deferred and multiplied as soon as one begins to
interpret.

In fact Miller goes on from this passage to pick up a metaphor
from Hardy which has since become something of an *idée fixe* in
his deconstructionist writing. Indulging his penchant for riddling etymologies, Miller reminds us of the affinity between

'text', 'texture' and the 'tissue' of associative links which relate writing to the language of weaving and tapestry.

> The critic adds his weaving to the Penelope's web of the text, or unravels it so that its structuring threads may be laid bare, or re-weaves it, or traces out one thread in the text to reveal the design it inscribes . . . (ibid.)

This labyrinthine imagery and play on language are typical of Hillis Miller's way with deconstruction. For him, as for Hartman, it combines a certain devious rigour of explanation with an even more attractive strangeness of result. It also manages to solve at a stroke those problems of consciousness *vis-à-vis* the text which beset Miller's earlier criticism. If interpretation is always caught up in a chain of proliferating sense which it can neither halt nor fully comprehend, then the critic is effectively absolved of all responsibility for limiting the play of his own imagination. This means a total break with the notions of fidelity and disciplined awareness enjoined by Miller's Genevan mentors. By replacing the rhetoric of consciousness with a rhetoric of textuality, deconstruction – at least as Miller conceives it – obliterates the line between text and interpretation.

In their day the New Critics would have stigmatized such talk as a bad case of the 'personalist heresy', the mistake of treating criticism as a vehicle or platform for displays of interpretative brilliance. W. K. Wimsatt, philosopher-elect of the movement, played on this theme in a rearguard defence of New Critical precepts (Wimsatt 1970). Unless it preserved some sense of the poem as an autonomous object – in Hegel's terms, a 'concrete universal' – interpretation would always be tempted to run wild in games of its own inventing. Hence the title of Wimsatt's essay ('Battering the Object'), and hence his choice of Hillis Miller, among others, as an influence to be held at bay.

At the time it was Miller's Genevan connections and his subjectivist approach which seemed to Wimsatt a dangerous sign of critical malaise. And in a sense his predictions were accurate enough, as Miller and Hartman went on to prove. Wimsatt's essay makes every attempt to counter the threatened dissolution of boundaries between text and criticism. The idea of 'organic form', he observes, was 'a very material subject-matter (as in Erasmus Darwin's "Botanical Garden") . . .

before it became the rarified metaphysics of a theory of aesthetic knowledge and form' (ibid., p. 63). By this rather offbeat comparison Wimsatt clearly means to defend the New Critical idea of the poem as a self-contained 'organic' form, as opposed to those critics – like Hartman and Hillis Miller – who were busily deconstructing such claims. He is even prepared to welcome those aspects of structuralist thought that can be turned to advantage in propping up the notion of textual autonomy. Thus Wimsatt quotes approvingly Jakobson's famous statement that poetic language 'projects the principle of equivalence from the axis of selection onto the axis of combination' (ibid., p. 78). This has the merit, in Wimsatt's eyes, of focusing attention on the self-sufficient formal attributes of poetry, rather than trying to dissolve them (like Miller) into the play of interpretative consciousness. The fact that he can enlist Jakobson as an ally for 'the ontological approach' is evidence of the deep affinity between New Critical poetics and structuralism in its classic, conservative form.

The Yale deconstructors reject this ontological constraint and happily embrace all the dangers Wimsatt so strenuously sought to avoid. Hartman makes a virtue and even a vocation of pushing his critical style to the edge of sheer self-indulgence. His recent collection of essays (*Criticism in the Wilderness*, 1980) is a plea for critics to 'come out' and stake their claim to an answerable style released from the old New Critical conventions of sobriety and tact. Behind Hartman's case is a rootedly American dislike of what he calls 'the Arnoldian concordat', the view of criticism as at best a humble handmaid to creative endeavour. He sees this attitude as having passed down through Eliot to the American New Critics, enforcing an orthodox code of interpretative manners which reflects the continuing dominance in America of British tradition. For Hartman the problem of critical style is closely bound up with the question of cultural identity and the need, as he sees it, to establish a distinctively 'American' voice for criticism. This in turn goes along with an openness to continental European sources – Heidegger, Derrida, Walter Benjamin, and others – not so much for their specific ideas as for the fact that they fly in the face of everything 'British' and post-Eliotic.

Hartman's enterprise takes courage, as well it might, from

Derrida's deconstructive merging of origin and supplement, or text and commentary. Criticism is now 'crossing over' into literature, rejecting its subservient, Arnoldian stance and taking on the freedom of interpretative style with a matchless gusto. Theory becomes, in Hartman's hands, a tactical weapon of provocative intent against all those self-imposed restrictions that critics have hitherto embraced. The result is a striking but rather promiscuous line-up of names and philosophies. Hartman is even ready to defend the obfuscating rant of Thomas Carlyle, finding it a salutary antidote to the suave complacencies of Arnold. In the Yale revisionists (especially Harold Bloom) he perceives the same hankering for a language true to its prophetic lights and possessing the courage of its metaphors. Oscar Wilde's twists of paradox in 'The Critic as Artist' are set alongside the deconstructionist statements of Nietzsche, Heidegger and Derrida.

Hartman is not concerned to accommodate these thinkers to any kind of ordered or consistent philosophy. Indeed, the 'accommodating' style in criticism – the stress on good sense, rationality and order – is Hartman's main target in most of his recent essays. There has now grown up, he suggests,

> a new isolationism masking under the name of Common Sense and characterizing what it opposes as Skywriting. The Skywriters march under the banner of Hegel and continental philosophy, while the Common Sense school is content with no philosophy, unless it be that of Locke and a homespun organicism.   (Hartman 1978, p. 409)

The pretence of even-handedness here is shrewdly undermined by the choice of metaphors. Hartman himself is a confirmed Skywriter, drawing all his sources behind him in the same meteoric orbit.

This is deconstruction 'on the wild side', a criticism that thrives on Derrida's example but rarely seeks to emulate his rigour of argument. Hartman can defend his all-embracing rhetoric by invoking Derrida's powerful deconstructions of philosophic texts. From here it is a short step to the general idea that philosophy is simply another variety of literature, a text pervaded by the same ruses of figuration. In which case, Hartman concludes, 'It is not a matter of "knowing" Derrida or

Heidegger but of reading and steeping oneself in a corpus of critical, philosophical, and literary texts that they incorporate and revise' (ibid., p. 411). Thus Hartman justifies his attempt to wrench criticism away from its humble destiny by exposing it to all the buffeting philosophic winds he can raise. Taking the rigorous work of deconstruction largely for granted, Hartman frolics in the aftermath with great stylistic verve and a thankful sense of having moved, for his part, decisively 'beyond formalism'.

Yet nagging doubts remain about Hartman's breezy assurance that 'knowing' Derrida or Heidegger is less important than bathing in their heady rhetorical wake. His strategies, even more than Miller's, run up against a sticking-point which recalls – ironically – Wimsatt's principled stand on the question of objectivity. Hartman's essay 'The Interpreter' closes on the following typically extravagant but queasy note:

> Things get mixed up in this jittery situation. It should be the interpreter who unfolds the text. But the book begins to question the questioner, its *qui vive* challenges him to prove he is not a ghost. What is he then?   (Hartman 1975, p.19)

The reference, of course, is to *Hamlet*, and Hartman obligingly goes on to transpose the dialogue:

> *Interpreter:* Who's there?
> *Book:* Nay, answer me; stand, and unfold yourself.

Hartman clearly enjoys these perplexities and exploits them, as here, to paradoxical effect. On the other hand they do remain fixed at a level of self-occupied rhetorical juggling which never really breaks with the old antinomies created by formalist dogma. Hartman's impressionistic style is trapped in an endless rehearsal of gestures which raise the 'personalist heresy' to a high point of philosophic principle. In the last analysis his criticism moves not so much 'beyond formalism' as round and about its ambiguous fringes.

Paul de Man: rhetoric and reason

If Hartman represents deconstruction in its ludic or libertarian vein, Paul de Man exemplifies the opposite qualities of hard-pressed argument and high conceptual rigour. In his Preface to the collective volume *Deconstruction and Criticism* (1979), Hartman divides the Yale revisionists into two broad categories of 'canny' and 'uncanny' critics, the latter being those (Paul de Man among them) who pursue deconstruction to its ultimate, unsettling conclusions. In fact one could argue that these terms cross over and exchange implications in truly Derridean style. De Man is in a sense the 'canniest' of all, since he exerts a firm argumentative grasp, even at the furthest reaches of paradox, and never permits himself anything like Hartman's style of rhapsodic philosophizing.

We have already seen how de Man's rhetorical strategies were applied to the 'old' New Criticism and its organicist metaphors. Unlike Hartman, he is not content with a skirmishing engagement, a mode of deconstruction that lives on its wits and offers no hold for theory. De Man's readings draw out the innermost logic of the text, showing how figurative tensions develop to a point where that logic is implicitly confounded by its own implications. For de Man this discrepancy between reason and rhetoric is endemic to all literary texts, and to criticism also wherever it passes from mere explication to theory and self-conscious method: 'Critics' moments of greatest blindness with regard to their own critical assumptions are also the moments at which they achieve their greatest insights' (de Man 1971, p. 109). This leads on to the argument that texts always generate a history of partial or 'aberrant' readings, the blindspots of which can be deconstructed but never so completely demystified as to bring criticism out on a level of perfect clarity and truth. 'Criticism' and 'crisis' are linked not only by a punning etymology but by the very nature of interpretative thought. 'The rhetoric of crisis states its own truth in the mode of error' (ibid., p. 16). This is to say that criticism thrives on an ultimate *aporia* which it may not recognize but which everywhere marks its performance.

De Man's most recent collection of essays (*Allegories of Reading*, 1979) started out, he says, as an 'historical study' but transformed itself along the way into a 'theory of reading'. How this came about can be seen most clearly in the chapter on Proust. Taking a passage from *Du Côté de chez Swann* which treats expressly of the pleasures of reading, de Man mounts an intricate critique which shows how the metaphors of 'inward contemplation' (literature as escape) are subtly intertwined with those of referential (or 'real-life') experience. This has the effect of breaking down the conventional assumption that draws a firm line between private and public activities, the world of thought and the world outside. Despite Proust's manifest intention, his images of solitary pleasure give way to a jostling crowd of apparently *external* sense-impressions. Perception and imagination are strangely confused, along with the normative logic that tries to hold them apart. Such 'static polarities', as de Man explains, are 'put into circulation by a more or less hidden system of relays which allows the properties to enter into substitutions, exchanges and crossings that appear to reconcile the incompatibilities of the inner with the outer world' (de Man 1979, p. 60). De Man pursues these figurative detours with a rigour of argument none the less 'logical' for its end result in paradox and *aporia*. The reading thus produced is unthinkable, he admits, in terms of a straightforward logic 'dominated by truth and error'. Yet the power of figurative language is such as to command our provisional assent to the 'totalizing world' that Proust's metaphors create.

De Man is all the same a 'canny' enough critic to glimpse, behind these metaphors, a kind of inbuilt textual unravelling which declares their subterfuge even in the act of rhetorically passing it off. Though there may be, as he says, 'no limit to what tropes can get away with', still there is an element of self-deconstruction involved in all such figurative language. Proust's metaphorical epiphanies always dissolve, under close inspection, into chains of 'literal' (or metonymic) detail which undercut the claim to a unified world of inward and outward perception.

Metaphor and metonymy are singled out by Roman Jakobson, and by many structuralist critics, as the two most pervasive and powerful devices of rhetorical language. Metaphor involves the perception of a similarity between two otherwise quite distinct fields of meaning, such that the sense of distance is preserved in the act of imaginatively leaping across it. The 'wind of change' is by now a metaphor staled by habit, but which still carries a sense of vaguely 'poetic' suggestion. For this reason metaphor has come to be regarded as the virtual hallmark of 'creative' language, the means by which it breaks with the normal run of day-to-day 'literal' usage. Metonymy, mean-while, works by substituting part for whole, 'the name of an attribute or adjunct . . . for that of the thing meant' (e.g. 'all hands on deck', where 'hands' refers metonymically to the men who have and use them). Thus in Yeats's lines from 'Leda and the Swan' –

> A shudder in the loins engenders there
> The broken wall, the burning roof and tower
> And Agamemnon dead.

the language involves both metaphor *and* metonymy, each sufficiently signalled by context. The 'broken wall' and 'burn-ing roof and tower' are aspects of a mind's-eye image of Troy which the reader supplies, as it were, to fill out the picture. To interpret 'a shudder in the loins' requires a larger stretch of imaginative reason, connecting the 'literal' sense (the rape of Leda) to various Yeatsian themes of historical catastrophe and violent rebirth. Metonymy is in this sense closer to what we think of as straightforward referential language. It has therefore been devalued by many rhetoricians as a device either subser-vient to metaphor or simply not requiring detailed explanation. The importance of Jakobson's distinction – as David Lodge argues in *The Modes of Modern Writing* (1977) – is that it treats metaphor and metonymy as equally resourceful but organized according to opposite schemes of production. Thus Lodge proposes a new kind of literary history, based on Jakobson's bi-polar model and tracing the periodic shifts of emphasis from strongly metaphorical (modernist) to markedly metonymic (or 'realistic') writing.

Lodge is perfectly at ease within the broad structuralist limits of applied theory and description. He is not concerned to deconstruct either his own working concepts or the texts that provide their testing-ground and justification. De Man's reflec-tions on metaphor and metonymy follow a very different path. Where Lodge treats the two devices as mapping out the field of modern writing – as if in a kind of amicable rivalry – de Man finds them everywhere locked in rhetorical combat. For him it is not enough to challenge traditional prejudice by placing metonymy on an equal footing with the claims of metaphor. Their relationship needs to be totally reversed, so that metaphor displays a delusory, at times almost furtive, attempt to cover its own textual workings. Hence the demystifying power that de Man seeks out in texts, like those of Proust, which lay bare the sources of illusion. The seductions of metaphor cannot, in the end, disguise the figural means by which their effects are attained. A close enough reading always reveals the constitutive gap between intention and meaning. The actual workings of Proustian description are always at bottom metonymic, though 'motivated by a tendency to pretend the opposite'.

This suspension of language between metaphor and metonymy – or 'symbol' and 'discourse' – is the crux of de Man's interpretative theory. In *Blindness and Insight* it pointed the way towards deconstructing the organicist metaphors, the images of self-sufficient unity and form, prevalent among the American New Critics. The same oppositions are at work in de Man's various essays on the concepts of metaphor and symbol advanced by the Romantics (mainly Wordsworth and Coleridge) in their quest for a unified order of perception (see de Man 1969). Typically, de Man finds these concepts undone by a reading that interrogates their figures of encompassing vision – the symbol as a pure, intuitive merging of subject and object – and that sets in their place an open-ended 'allegory' of thought in the process of reflective understanding. This is the outcome of his essay on the German poet Rilke (in de Man 1979, pp. 20–56), where de Man explores the limits of a poetry devoted (as he reads it) to a rhetoric of 'pure figuration'. The failure to achieve this exemplary status – to redeem language from every last taint of its referential function – appears in the ruses and detours of meaning which Rilke is forced to exploit. It amounts to a virtual undoing of the perfect correspondence (implied but unachieved) between 'the semantic function and the formal structure of language'. Poetry succeeds in sustaining such high-Romantic themes 'only at the cost of a subterfuge to which it finds itself necessarily condemned'.

One is left in effect with a choice of readings, naïve or deconstructionist. Deconstruction suspends the persuasive (or meaningful) force of language in the interests of a purified logic of figure. The naïve reading yields itself, more or less consciously, to what de Man calls 'a normative pathos or ethical coercion'. While he admits that there must always be room for this latter possibility, de Man loads his terms so as to leave no doubt that deconstruction is the preferred alternative. To submit unresistingly to a 'normative pathos' or 'ethical coercion' is clearly not the way of critical intelligence as de Man conceives it. At times, indeed, there seems a kind of ethical compulsion behind the zeal with which he prosecutes the vagaries of symbol and metaphor. Frank Lentricchia has recently suggested (Lentricchia 1980) that de Man's criticism bears the marks of a lingering Sartrian influence, the existentialist concept of 'bad faith' being silently translated into textual-rhetorical terms. Metaphor and symbol would then correspond to the *mauvaise foi* of accepting human nature as something fixed and self-determined, its meaning given in advance. Deconstruction would set itself to prove, on the contrary, that meaning is produced (like Sartrian authenticity) only through a constant self-critique which always *defers* the sense of achieved identity. Certainly de Man is the fiercest of the Yale deconstructors, with a rigour not easily explained unless in ethical terms.

But de Man himself would be the last to claim that deconstruction carries on at an altitude of thought removed from all persuasive or ethical drives. His readings of Nietzsche make this point over and again. Nietzsche may dismiss the traditional idea of 'rhetoric as eloquence', and concentrate instead on the business of critically unravelling the tropes, revealing their false and presumptive claims to truth. But this enterprise itself requires a style of persuasive presentation which can scarcely elude the traps laid down by its own self-critical awareness. Nietzsche's critique of metaphysics, like Derrida's after him, has to be conducted in a language that partakes of both conceptual and persuasive elements. Its rhetoric belongs as much to 'literature' as to 'philosophy', so far as that distinction still holds up.

In fact, it is de Man's central argument here that 'literature' is precisely what results from philosophy's inability to *think through* its own constitution in textual-rhetorical terms. Nietzsche is a stylist, a 'literary' writer, to the extent that he acknowledges the ultimate complicity of thought and rhetoric, the fact that his critique of philosophy is itself 'structured as rhetoric'. Nietzsche in the end 'rehabilitates persuasion' by showing that language in its performative aspect both pervades and delimits the project of philosophy. The term 'performative' is taken from the philosopher J. L. Austin, who applied it to those forms of utterance (or 'speech-act') which are meant to produce effects – to persuade, promise, etc. – as opposed to purely assertive or 'constative' utterances. Nietzsche's rhetoric, according to de Man, 'earns a right' to its own inconsistency by pursuing the work of deconstruction to a point where knowledge encounters the absolute *need* for performative expression. (See pp. 108ff. for more detailed discussion of Austin and speech-act philosophy.)

Allegories of Reading can therefore be seen as an effort to negotiate – though not simply to conflate – the rival claims to knowledge of philosophy and literature. The habit of treating them as separate disciplines is one that, in de Man's view, 'deprives the reading of philosophical texts of elementary refinements that are taken for granted in literary interpretation'. But this is not merely – as it can seem with Hartman – a game of critical oneupmanship, a takeover bid on behalf of literary theory. De Man's 'canny' qualities of disciplined argument are sufficient guarantee against the kind of self-supporting intellectual romp that deconstruction sometimes seems to invite. Nietzsche, he remarks – and the same might be said of de Man's own writing – 'advocates the use of epistemologically rigorous methods as the only possible means to reflect on the limitations of those methods' (de Man 1979, p. 115). In the end it is only by confronting its limits – by forcing analysis to the point of *aporia* or self-contradiction – that thought comes up against the gap between itself and the aberrant 'logic' of the text.

Deconstruction at the limit?

Along with this respect for the protocols of reason, de Man shows an unusual willingness (unusual, that is, by deconstructionist standards) to credit the text with some implicit grasp of its own rhetorical strategies. This question first posed itself in the chapter on Rousseau in *Blindness and Insight*, where de Man effectively argued, as against Derrida, that a text must in some sense contain or *prefigure* its own deconstructive reading. It may be as Jonathan Culler has argued (1972), that de Man's was itself an oddly partial reading, one that ignored those passages where Derrida insists on the close and reciprocal exchange between text and deconstruction. But de Man has a real case to argue, and takes it up again, more resourcefully, in *Allegories of Reading*.

His contention is that rhetoric considered in the suasive (or performative) mode must finally escape the rigours of deconstruction. 'A statement of mistrust', as he puts it, 'is neither true nor false: it is rather in the nature of a permanent hypothesis.' Deconstruction can sustain its sceptical position only to the point where its findings have to be argued in more or less persuasive terms. And at this point, as Nietzsche perceived, it will always elude or controvert its own most vigilant scepticism. The interpreter faces the same dilemma. On the one hand, he can adopt a thoroughgoing sceptical line which detects and discounts every last vestige of a suasive rhetoric – in which case (as de Man shows of Derrida) his reading must open up an endless series of further deconstructions, each latching on to those rhetorical aspects that can never be expunged in its own performance. On the other hand, the critic can acknowledge, with de Man, that there must be an end-point to this dizzying regress. It is reached at the moment when scepticism encounters a figural will to power beyond reach of further deconstruction.

This is not, of course, the kind of 'intentionalist' reading which the old New Critics – and the structuralists after them – so firmly rejected. Without wishing to claim that Rousseau intended, or consciously grasped, any such latent possibilities of meaning, de Man puts the case that his *texts* in themselves provide the only starting-point for deconstructive treatment. This position is maintained against considerable odds in the chapters on Rousseau in *Allegories of Reading*. The odds are stacked by de Man himself, who goes to quite remarkable lengths to demonstrate the gap between Rousseau's apparent topics of discourse – culture, politics, his own life-history – and the textual dynamics that govern and (most often) undermine them. It is a case, once again, of the tropes taking over the business of narrative or logical argument, substituting a play of figural language that obeys its own laws of inverted cause-and-effect.

De Man is at his most 'uncanny' when describing the *Social*

Contract (for instance) as a text that refers not *outside itself* to some real political order but entirely to its own 'constitution' as a network of rhetorical codes and devices. As he puts it at one point,

> The tension between figural and grammatical language is duplicated in the differentiation between the State as a defined entity (État) and the State as a principle of action (Souverain) or, in linguistic terms, between the constative and the performative aspect of language.   (de Man 1979, p. 270)

As the *Contract* itself is both 'statutory and operative', so the language that describes it shuttles incessantly between constative and performative roles. The 'double perspective', in this case, involves an understanding that Rousseau's text both deconstructs its own argument and saves itself – like Nietzsche's – by a kind of preemptive rhetorical strike. Writing survives and transcends the process of figural reduction.

There is a similar, redemptive turn of argument in de Man's final chapter on Rousseau's *Confessions*. Here it is the nature of narrative 'excuses' – the fiction masquerading as honest self-scrutiny – which provides a handle for deconstructive reading. To 'confess' is to indulge in a series of self-justifying utterances which claim to be 'sincere', or to offer direct access to the writer's memories and conscience. Yet confessions are always, in some sense, a strategy designed to 'excuse' the penitent by placing his guilt in a narrative context that explains it, and thus dissolves responsibility. Such excuses run the danger that 'they will indeed exculpate the confessor, thus making the confession (and the confessional text) redundant as it originates' (ibid., pp. 278–301).

Again, there is a gap opened up between the claim to truth and the way in which the text deconstructs that claim as a merely rhetorical or *post hoc* rationalization. Guilt – including the 'guilty pleasure' of writing – can always be seen as a product of textual contrivance, re-created by a narrative cunning that evades, while ostensibly parading, the causes that engender it. Once embarked on his narrative, Rousseau is caught in a chain of signifying episodes that substitute their own devious logic for the truth-telling virtues of autobiography. So much so, indeed, that 'Rousseau's text, against its author's interest, prefers being suspected of lie and slander rather than of innocently lacking sense' (ibid., p. 293). The imperatives of writing subdue those of truth or candour, reducing the *Confessions* – from a deconstructive viewpoint – to 'a product of textual grammar or a radical fiction'.

This would seem to press as far as possible towards discounting intentions, or involving them in a web of textual significations beyond all conscious control. For de Man, however, the point is to recognize the fundamental urging of a rhetoric which nevertheless persists in the text when deconstruction has employed all the means at its disposal. Rousseau's 'excuses' may not function in the way he explicitly intends, but they still lead back to a conflict of motive and logic where the subtlest critic meets his match. Language itself, in de Man's words, 'dissociates the cognition from the act'. What the text *performs* is in the last analysis immune from further sceptical attack. Deconstruction is not a matter of mere critical gamesmanship precisely because it uses – *can* only use – the figural leads and devices advanced by the text itself. In reading, as de Man insists, we are 'only trying to come closer to being as rigorous a reader as the author had to be in order to write the sentence in the first place'. It is to this end of saving the text that de Man so carefully stakes out the limits of deconstruction and the gap that persists between the reductive grammar of tropes and the rhetoric of textual performance.

'Ordinary language': the challenge from Austin

Derrida himself – it must be said – gives little sign of accepting any such 'performative' check to the free play of deconstruction. His treatment of speech-act philosophy, in the essay 'Signature Event Context' (Derrida 1977b), sparked off an exchange with the American philosopher John Searle, in the course of which Derrida made it plain that his intent was to baffle and provoke, rather than to reach any common ground of discussion. The essay itself (first published in French) is rigorously argued and takes up many of the themes familiar from *Of Grammatology*. The rejoinder to Searle is in a very different vein, playing all manner of mock-solemn games with Searle's line of argument and no doubt indulging the Yale deconstructors in their taste for such verbal jousting. It is clear from this exchange that Derrida has absorbed more than a little of the ludic propensity shown by his American disciples (Paul de Man excepted). His encounter, first with speech-act philosophy and then with Searle as its living representative, offers a measure of this tactical-cultural shift.

'Signature Event Context' is mainly concerned with Austin's theory of performative utterance, as briefly described above. According to Austin, language serves a great variety of purposes, not all of which are accountable as statements of fact or logical entailment (see Austin 1963). It can be used to *perform* certain kinds of rhetorical act like promising, declaring a couple man and wife, or ritually naming some object or other. Such performative functions may be explicitly marked ('I *hereby* declare . . .'), or they may depend on context for their special meaning. What sets them apart from statements of fact is the *intention* or 'illocutionary force' (Austin's term) which goes along with their utterance. Performatives involve an intention and a commitment, on the speaker's part, to stand by his words and acknowledge (at least as he utters them) all the obligations they entail.

Austin introduces various refinements and distinctions by way of explaining the different kinds of illocutionary force. Common to them all, however, is the idea that performative speech-acts are somehow guaranteed and authenticated by the present good faith of whoever utters them. Austin expressly rules out such 'etiolated' or 'parasitic' instances as promises spoken in jest, on the stage, or as part of a quotation from some source other than the speaker. These utterances are void of commitment, merely aping the conventions and in no sense possessing genuine performative status. The conditions of producing a 'felicitous' speech-act – on Austin's terms – can be summarized as sincerity, correctness of form, and propriety of context. To fail on any of these counts is to fall into idle talk or other, more insidious kinds of linguistic delinquency.

Derrida finds in Austin's notion of 'speech-act' a classic restatement of the philosophic stance that privileges 'speech' at the expense of 'writing'. Austin's conditions of performative felicity require that the speaker 'mean what he says' in the sense of being presently involved with his utterance and faithfully *intending* its import. Yet it is in the very nature of performatives, Derrida argues, that they hold good for various occasions and contexts where the supposed original force of intention is no longer present. Performative speech-acts derive their operative meaning from the fact that they embody *conventional* forms and tokens of utterance which are always already in existence before the speaker comes to use them. This 'iterability', or power of being transferred from one specific context to another, is evidence that speech-acts cannot be confined to the unique self-present moment of meaning. They partake of the *differance* or distancing from origin that marks all language in so far as it exceeds and pre-exists the speaker's intention. Austin's criteria for speech-act felicity are therefore inconsistent with what his performatives are actually required to do. They manifest the same metaphysical hankering for presence and origins that Derrida discerns in the texts of Saussure or Husserl. The 'iterability' of performatives means that they can be explained and located only within a larger system of non-self-present signification. They belong to *writing* in Derrida's sense of the word: an economy of difference nowhere coinciding with the present intentions of individual speech.

This gives Derrida his hold for deconstructing those loaded oppositions that Austin requires in order to separate 'felicitous' from 'infelicitous' speech-acts. Does it not follow, Derrida asks,

> that what Austin excludes as anomaly, exception, 'non-serious', *citation* (on stage, in a poem, or a soliloquy) is the determined modification of a general citationality – or rather, a general iterability – without which there would not even be a 'successful' speech-act?   (Derrida 1977b, p. 191)

The same applies to signatures, including Derrida's own, artfully appended to this essay. Signatures confer an authenticity which, depending as it does on *repetition* – on the capacity for being detached from 'the present and singular intention' of the signatory – always lies open to doubt. The 'felicitous' signing of a cheque, for instance, depends on certain agreed preconditions of trust, mainly the signatory's knowledge – or conviction – that the bank will honour his requirement. Yet the very conventionality of such transactions leaves them perpetually exposed to fraud and double-dealing, just as language may often not 'mean what it says'.

Of course, Derrida concedes, we get along normally without entertaining such doubts, accepting the conventions of authenticity as if they belonged to a natural order of truth. Their 'effects' in day-to-day discourse can hardly be questioned. But to build a whole *philosophy* on the conventions of language, as Austin does, is to invite a more rigorous scrutiny – one that uncovers contradictions in the nature of speech-act commitment. As Derrida argues, these 'effects' are only made possible by a repressed knowledge that the opposite could always obtain, that they may be grounded in nothing more than an empty or fallible convention. The underlying metaphors of Austin's philosophy – 'pure' versus 'impure' speech-acts, 'parasitical' variants, and so forth – are highly susceptible of deconstruction.

Searle responds to the effect that Derrida has confused the issue, mainly by ignoring the communicative ground-rules that give performative language its particular force (Searle 1977). His argument rests on the Chomskian assumption that speakers possess an innate linguistic competence by which they are enabled to produce and comprehend a potentially infinite variety of well-formed utterances. From this point of view the conventionality of speech-acts is precisely the means of their being understood and preserving their force *despite* the vicissitudes of context. Searle thus reverses Derrida's argument, maintaining that the 'iterability' of linguistic forms 'facilitates and is a necessary condition of the forms of intentionality that are characteristic of speech-acts' (ibid., p. 208). He further objects that Derrida's concept of 'writing' ignores the basic intelligibility that attaches to most written texts irrespective of whether the author's 'intentions' are there to consult. Communicative competence plays the same role in written as in spoken language, allowing the reader – if he is not intent upon wilful obfuscation – to apply the standard interpretative rules and arrive at the intended conclusion. Searle thus rejects the Derridean claim that speech-acts are invaded by a 'generalized citationality' (or writing) which renders them just as 'parasitic' as the deviant cases proscribed by Austin.

Clearly this exchange held out small promise of agreement or concession on either side. Searle presupposes what Derrida denies to begin with: that language is properly adapted to communicate meaning, and – as a corollary to this – that whatever obstructs communication is either deviant or somehow beside the point. Derrida opens his essay by deconstructing the very concept of 'communication', arguing that it opens into regions of undecidability where no appeal to context or convention can possibly arrest the disseminating free play of language. The sheer distance of thought between Derrida and Searle can be gauged by an example the latter gives to support his view of communicative competence. 'On the twentieth of September 1793 I set out on a journey from London to Oxford' (ibid., p. 20). Now here, Searle argues, is a straightforward communication which comes across plainly, despite the fact that the author and his 'intentions' are long since dead. Searle puts this example forward as a knock-down case which presumably even Derrida could hardly controvert.

But such sentences are favoured 'texts' for deconstruction, not only by Derrida but by others (like Barthes) who share his fascination with the slippages of everyday referential meaning. Barthes quotes the merest of telegraphic greetings: 'Monday. Returning tomorrow. Jean-Louis.' He then makes play with all the possible ambiguities that lurk behind even such a simple and practical piece of language. (*Which* Jean-Louis? *Which* of the various Mondays on which the message might have been penned?) From this point Barthes takes off into one of those flights of strange but meticulously argued fantasy that characterize his later writing. Society, he reflects, tries to bar such pleasurable vagaries by insisting on specific memoranda of dates, places, patronymics, and so forth. But can we not imagine

> the freedom and, so to speak, the erotic fluidity . . . which would speak only in pronouns and shifters, each person never saying anything but *I*, *tomorrow*, *over there*, without referring to anything legal whatsoever, and in which the *vagueness of difference* (the only fashion of respecting its subtlety) would be language's most precious value?   (Barthes 1977, pp. 165–6)

What Barthes is imagining here is the utopian equivalent of Derrida's *differance*, a pure textuality redeemed from every last taint of referential meaning. It is a view of language undreamt of in Searle's philosophy because it totally rejects the normative constraints of effective communication. Where Searle rests squarely on commonsense assumptions about how words are *used* in everyday practical terms, Derrida and Barthes see language as everywhere revealing its potential aberrations and never coming to rest in a stable order of meaning.

In his subsequent rejoinder, 'Limited Inc abc' (Derrida 1977c), Derrida exploits every possible means of subverting the logic and tacit assumptions behind Searle's argument. He makes great play with the notion of copyright, incorporating large chunks of Searle's text – indeed, during the course of his argument, quoting all of it! – and turning them against their own purpose by manifold sleights of cunning. In what sense can Searle have proprietory interest in a text that claims to be founded on truths universally implicit in the nature of language? Derrida even renames his opponent 'SARL', the spelling of which is meant to indicate 'Société à responsabilité limitée', or 'Limited' (company) or 'Inc', as the title has it. Searle/Sarl is thus set up as a convenient butt for Derrida's attack on the notion that texts can be owned, controlled, 'limited' or appropriated in the name of some legitimating authorial source. The exchange becomes, for Derrida, an elaborate cross-play of textual strategies and in no sense an encounter of two self-possessed philosophical views. He goes on to exercise a shrewd deconstructive leverage on all those concepts and protocols of argument that Searle accepts as a basis for 'serious' discussion. What is left of speech-act philosophy if one chooses to question the ethics of sincerity and speaking-in-earnest which it has to presuppose? Searle's passing reference to the 'suspect status of the "non-serious"' gives Derrida an opening for much delighted play with the solemn conventions of Anglo-American academic discourse. Searle adopts a sternly proprietory tone in pointing out Derrida's 'misunderstandings' of speech-act philosophy, his 'falsification' of the issues involved and the fact that 'Derrida's Austin . . . bears almost no relation to the original'. Such arguments fall completely into Derrida's hands, assuming as they do that 'Austin' is not just the name attached to a certain body of texts but that Austin's presence – and that of his disciple – continues to exercise a sovereign power over how those texts are to be read.

Derrida is under no illusion that he has 'taken Sarl seriously' or met his arguments with reasoned opposition at any point. The object of 'Limited Inc' is to stage a confrontation which never really takes place, but the very *avoidance* of which is a kind of tactical triumph. Derrida's aim throughout is to manoeuvre Searle on to textual ground where speech-act conventions run up against absurdity or limiting cases of their own application. As he archly suggests at one point,

> a theoretician of speech-acts who was even moderately con-
> sistent with his own theory ought to have spent some time
> patiently considering questions of this type: Does the prin-
> cipal purpose [of 'Signature Event Context'] consist in being
> *true*? In appearing true? In stating the truth?
>   And what if *SEC* were *doing something else*?   (Derrida 1977c,
> p. 178)

That 'something else' is deconstruction in the 'uncanny' or vertiginous mode Derrida has often exploited when writing for a mainly American readership. Its themes are certainly con-tinuous with his earlier texts, but its strategies more artfully contrived, more roundabout and circumstantial.

It would clearly be rash in the extreme, after Derrida's exchange with Searle, to suppose that these ludic elements exclude any 'serious' intent. On the other hand it is interesting to see how Derrida's texts have been drawn and provoked by their involvement with American debates. A striking example is Derrida's contribution to the volume *Deconstruction and Criticism*, published as a kind of manifesto for the Yale deconstructionists (Hartman 1979). The topic is ostensibly Shelley's poem 'The Triumph of Life', which serves as a focus for the other contribu-tors but which barely manages to peep through the tangles and cunning indirections of Derrida's text. He makes no pretence of 'interpreting' the poem but uses its title and random associative hints as a springboard into regions of giddying uncertainty, where details merge and cross in a joyful breakdown of all proprietory limits. Any talk of meaning or structure is ineluct-ably 'caught up in a process which it does not control', which for Derrida signals the total dissolution of those boundaries that mark off one text from another, or that try to interpose between poem and commentary. 'The Triumph of Life' is teasingly played off against Blanchot's narrative *L'Arrêt de mort*, producing a series of figurative crossings and wild substitutions which abolish all sense of textual autonomy. This gambit is pushed to the limit by a footnote, addressed to the translator, which runs the full length of Derrida's text and constantly adverts to the impossible nature of the whole undertaking – the way in which translation exemplifies the 'abysmal' slippages and detours of all understanding.

Derrida's strategy here has more in common with Hartman or Hillis Miller than with a 'purist' deconstructor like de Man. It is a virtuoso exercise of writing which assumes all the textual freedoms granted by an underdetermined or radically ambiguous context. Translation, like criticism, reaches a point where it has to abandon the manageable rhetoric of 'polysemia' (or multiple meaning, New Critical style) and embrace the 'free play' of textual dissemination. In his recent productions Derrida has used all the means at his disposal to project and *dramatize* this process, as distinct from the kind of rigorous argumentation at work in *Of Grammatology* or *Writing and Difference*. Of the critics at Yale it is de Man who has done most to sustain that early-Derridean insistence on the need for deconstruction to remain, in some sense, a discipline of close reading. Hartman's has been the more typical reaction, taking Derrida's texts as a cue for simply throwing off all the old, irksome restraints of method and style. To sort out the two-way 'influence' here would be a fruitless undertaking, given the degree of intertextual penetration and exchange which these writings consciously exploit. At any rate it is clear by now that deconstruction in America is not a monolithic theory or school of thought but a gathering-point for critics who are otherwise divided on many central questions of technique and style. Resistances and tensions are building at Yale, as they did during the waning of the 'old' New Criticism, presided over by Hartman and his colleagues. One of the most eloquent dissenting voices is that of Harold Bloom, whose strategies in the face of deconstruction have a strange heroic grandeur of their own.

Harold Bloom

We have seen how the challenge to formalist dogma went along with a revived interest in the poetry and ethos of Romanticism. Bloom devoted his first book to Shelley (*Shelley's Mythmaking*, 1959), who had long been the target of critics (Eliot and Allen Tate among them) who argued implicitly from Shelley's romanticized politics to what they considered his failings of imaginative nerve and moral immaturity. Shelley became the standard example of a poet who consistently overstepped the limits of answerable style and sacrificed his craft to the attractions of a vague pantheistical uplift or ersatz religion. T. E. Hulme had indeed stigmatized Romanticism as 'spilt religion', and laid down that poetry must not concern itself with ultimate issues beyond its proper scope and command. It was left to the New Critics to work out the systematic rules and sanctions of this moral embargo.

Bloom conducts a defence of Shelley which is also a principled rejection of the classicist poetic and everything that flowed from it. He develops an idea from the Jewish theologian Martin Buber, that human experience divides into two kinds or qualities – expressed in terms of the 'it' and 'thou' attitudes – which between them stake out the great moral choices of existence. Bloom sees Shelley as having tried over and again, in the best of his poetry, to reassert the value of human relationships, the 'thou'-saying attitude which creates a world of mutual recognition and sympathy, whether between man and man or man and the living universe. This amounts to an aesthetic philosophy opposed point for point to the formalist idea of the poem as an impersonal object or 'verbal icon' for detached contemplation. To Bloom's way of thinking, it is only in moments of emotional defeat – or satirical bitterness – that Shelley is forced back into such an impersonal mode. His case against Shelley's modern detractors rests on a neo-Romantic belief that the poet is indeed, as Wordsworth expressed it, 'a man speaking to men'. Critics who condemn the poetry on that account – under cover of formalist dogma – are simply closing their minds to any possibility of a world redeemed from the 'it-ness' of routine perception.

In Bloom's more recent writing the personalist heresy is

pushed even further in the direction of a full-blown Romantic myth of creation. *The Anxiety of Influence* (1973) laid the groundwork of Bloom's revisionist poetic. There exists, he argued, a complex and fascinating tension between the 'strong' poets in any tradition – those with a powerful drive to preserve their own identity – and the predecessor poets whose influence they have to cope with and somehow turn to advantage. The poet suffers with peculiar anguish that guilt-ridden hatred of the father that Freud detected at the root of family relations. His will to expression is pursued through cunning forms of displacement, or defensive 'tropes', which at the same time disguise and elaborate the will to be self-begotten, to acknowledge no previous authority or influence. The strong poet has the courage to recognize his own belatedness *vis-à-vis* the tradition he inherits, and the strength to subvert it by 'troping' his predecessors. How this theory might apply to the *woman* poet – since its terms are on the face of it so exclusively Oedipal – remains very much an open question, and one which Bloom never addresses.

From Spenser, through Milton to Blake, Shelley and such moderns as Lawrence and Yeats – the tradition Bloom stakes out is a line very different from that proposed by Eliot and the New Critics. Bloom's is a dissident tradition, which he traces back largely to the radical Protestant stirrings of the English Civil War, and which then reaches forward to the young Romantics and their thwarted hopes for the French Revolution. As Bloom points out, it is a line strategically ignored by Eliot and his followers, whose version of literary history – Donne, Herbert, Pope, Dr Johnson, Hopkins and Eliot himself – represents a distinctly Anglo-Catholic and conservative scheme of values. Bloom makes no bones about his preferences: 'One line, and it is the central one, is Protestant, radical and Miltonic-Romantic; the other is Catholic, conservative and, by its claims, classical.' There is a clear enough alignment between the latter tradition, with its emphasis on poetic self-discipline, and the working methods of formalist criticism. Bloom sets out not only to revise the whole modern estimate of poets such as Blake and Shelley but to reinstruct critics in the calling to which – as avatars of the same tradition – they are bound eventually to return.

Criticism for Bloom is a kind of poetic re-enactment, and he

shows small patience with the modest conventions of critical
address. *The Anxiety of Influence* presents an exotic terminology
and system of 'revisionary ratios' by which to plot the labyrinthine ruses of imaginative reason. In *Kabbalah and Criticism*
(Bloom 1975) the esoteric tonings are yet more insistent and
the claims more defiantly pitched. Drawing on the cabbalistic
mysteries of Creation, and all the attendant apparatus of
hermetic commentary, Bloom sets out a programme for criticism which could scarcely be further removed from the orthodox
Eliotic standpoint! The inspirational detours of cabbalistic
wisdom are equated with the acts of creative 'misprision', or
swerves from origin, which Bloom sees at work in all great
poetry. Whether or not these far-fetched analogies are really
worth the carriage depends on one's willingness to accept his
extraordinary claims for the saving power of poetic imagination.

Poetry and Repression (1976) finds Bloom once again on the
hallowed revisionary ground of Romantic and post-Romantic
poetry. 'Repression', for Bloom, is a word that moves across
suggestively from its Freudian sense of sublimated motive to a
meaning that also involves the sublime, but in a context more
familiar from Romantic philosophies of mind and nature. The
theme of a natural innocence regained is one that haunted the
imaginations of all those poets, from Blake to Wallace Stevens,
whose 'belatedness' Bloom sets out to interpret. The Romantic
sublime is a quest for lost origins which the strong poet always
engages in, though aware that his belated condition puts it
beyond reach of any but the subtlest tropes and displacements.
Repression is a knowledge of perpetual self-defeat, yet at the
same time a power of somehow retrieving the sublime through
the crises and conflicts of sublimated influence.

Up to a point there is much in common between Bloom's
'revisionary ratios' and the practice of deconstruction. Both
start out from the idea that literary history, in so far as it exists in
any genuine sense, has to deal with texts in their relationships
one with another, through a process of perpetual displacement
which can only be described in rhetorical terms. Both dismiss
the subjectivist illusion of the poet as self-possessed creator of
meaning, an individual subject expressing the truths of his own
authentic vision. To interpret a text is to seek out the strategies

and defensive tropes by which it either confronts or evades the texts that precede it. Bloom is in accord with Derrida when he insists that textual origins are always pushed back beyond recall, in a series of hard-fought rhetorical encounters that make up the line of descent in poetic history. Where the difference emerges is in Bloom's countervailing argument that the 'strong' poet must always strive to create at least a working-space of presence for his own imagination. In other words, Bloom wants to halt the process of deconstruction at a point where it is still possible to gauge a poet's creative stature in terms of his overriding will to expression. It could hardly be otherwise, given Bloom's intense involvement with Romantic poetry, and his efforts to rescue that tradition from the classicizing canon of Eliot and his followers.

It is therefore not surprising that in his recent books Bloom should seem torn between a defence of poetry which holds to the ethos of Romantic individualism, and a deconstructive poetics which tends to dissolve such themes into something approaching an abstract system of tropes and relationships. In the last resort, however, Bloom is always willing to invoke the terminology of 'voice', 'presence' and subjective origin which Derrida so resolutely tracks down to its metaphors. Bloom's arguments are mustered in his methodological 'coda' to *Wallace Stevens: The Poems of Our Climate* (1977). The book sets out to place Stevens's poetry in the great Romantic line of descent, which Bloom wants to claim as a modern American home-ground, since Eliot effectively broke with that tradition for English poets of a modernist sympathy. Behind this rejuvenated Romanticism stands the figure of Ralph Waldo Emerson, the Concord philosopher and sage whom Bloom regards as the great precursor of everything strongest and most vital in American poetry. Emerson becomes the mediating presence in a mode of pragmatic idealism which transplants the 'sublime' of Wordsworth and Shelley to a climate of belatedness and strenuous new beginnings. Emerson is shrewdly beforehand with the modern deconstructors by accepting from the outset the absence of comforting illusions – the bankruptcy of Idealism – and setting in their place a radical will to imaginative power. Stevens enters this picture as a poet of intense moral vision and 'humanizing pathos', whose relation to the American sublime involves him in a rhetoric of crisis, a sequence of urgently redemptive tropes and misprisions.

Bloom is here conducting a complex and many-levelled strategy of argument. He stands in much the same relation to his 'deconstructing' colleagues as Stevens to Emerson, or to that side of Emerson which wanted to reduce the expressiveness of language to the inbred tropes of rhetoric. 'Deconstructing Emerson is of course impossible, since no discourse has ever been so overtly aware of its status as rhetoricity' (Bloom 1977, p. 12). Faced with this impasse, Stevens adopts the only possible adequate response, a rhetoric strong enough to 'trope' or wilfully transfigure the Emersonian reduction. As Bloom most succinctly puts it:

> In Stevens, we will see Emersonian Fate turning into . . . the First Idea. Transcendental Freedom in Stevens becomes the refusal to bear so dehumanizing a reduction. Power or Will in Stevens' mature poetry is the reimagining of a First Idea.   (ibid., p. 27)

Bloom clearly sees himself as doing for present-day criticism what Stevens achieved for American poetry. His closing chapter confronts the deconstructors with an account of what it is to move *through* and *beyond* their doubting epistemology, to a concept of rhetoric that would reinstate the poet as a seeker after truths of his own strong imagining. Bloom still admits the power of deconstruction, the force of what he calls 'this advanced critical consciousness, the most rigorous and scrupulous in the field today'. But he sees no way beyond such a reductive outlook, except by readmitting the will to expression which animates not only the poet's tropes but the critic's rhetorical motives when he comes to interpret them. There has to be a leap from the knowledge that *all* interpretation is a network of superimposed tropes, to the faith that something might yet be achieved to clear a space for the modern imagination.

This is where Bloom parts company with de Man and the purist deconstructors. He sees them as having reached the point where scepticism must give way to a redemptive or reconstructive 'troping' aware of its own liabilities.

The issue of the limits of deconstruction will be resolved only

> if we attain a vision of rhetoric more comprehensive than the
> deconstructors allow, that is, if we can learn to see rhetoric as
> transcending the epistemology of tropes and re-entering the
> space of the will-to-persuasion.   (ibid., p. 387)

This act of willed reversal is the key-point of Bloom's poetics,
and the crux of his difference with Hartman, Miller and the
others. Powerful and convincing though their arguments are, it
is still possible to 'trope' them in turn by seeing their negative
stance as one stage only in a double movement of interpretative
thought. Bloom stakes his readings on a concept of 'misprision',
or masterful troping, which attempts this Nietzschean transvaluation of values. If the 'strong' poet is one who creatively
misreads and reinterprets the precursor, then the strength of
criticism is likewise its power to invest the strategies of reading
with a sense of hard won significance. This leads Bloom back to
the crisis-laden rhetoric of *Kabbalah and Criticism*, the argument of which he resumes in his closing pages on Stevens.
Cabbalistic tradition is quarried as a source of figurative ploys
sufficiently strange and powerful to confront the reductive
tropes of deconstruction.

One could hardly wish for a wilder and stranger language
than the rhetoric of 'crossings', or defensive encounters, which
Bloom brings to bear in his grappling with Stevens's poetry. It
is a language torn between the abstract register of post-
structuralist thought and the high prophetic tone of which
Bloom is both master and (occasionally) near-comic victim. He
takes the line of maximum resistance in straddling the ground
between thought and vision, concept and trope, philosophy and
poetry. His defence for this outlandish style is that it answers to
the strangeness and taxing rhetoric of poetry itself. Poets, he
argues, are first and foremost 'masters of misprision', and only
incidentally (or at a great remove of theory) the 'conceptual
rhetoricians' that deconstruction would make of them. To read
them 'more truly and more strange' we need in the end 'a wilder
definition of trope' than anything offered by the current deconstructors.

Bloom's real quarrel with his Yale colleagues is that they fail
to understand the conflicts and antagonisms engendered by the
poet's 'belated' encounter with tradition. The New Critics

invented various ways of sealing the poem off within a timeless, self-sufficient realm of interlocked meaning and structure. Internal 'tensions' (of irony, paradox, etc.) were there to validate the techniques of criticism as a disciplined and *sui generis* form of knowledge. Deconstruction abandons this fenced-off critical estate when it speaks of the 'intertextuality', or rhetoric of endlessly shuttling allusion, which makes up the history of writing. For Bloom, however, this notion is too generalized and neutral to convey the complex rivalries between poet and poet. If the New Critics sought to contain those tensions within the artificial limits of the poem-as-object, deconstruction seeks to dissolve them entirely by an open-ended rhetoric of pure figuration.

Bloom's appeal to cabbalistic doctrine is a means of countering both these reductions. At the heart of his poetics is the guiding assumption 'that a Kabbalistic or Gnostic theory of rhetoric must deny that there can be any *particular* semantic tension in language, because in the Kabbalistic vision all language is nothing but semantic tension raised to apocalyptic pitch'.   (ibid., p. 394). The 'particular tension' to which Bloom here refers might be glossed as the kind of specialized inbred rhetoric of poetry devised by the 'old' New Critics. At the same time his argument shrewdly undermines the deconstructionist position by insisting on the conflict of wills to expression behind the encounter of text with text. This struggle, he urges, must not be lost sight of in the undifferentiated merging or 'free play' envisaged by Derridean deconstruction.

Derrida and Bloom on Freud

Bloom is equally un-Derridean in the use he makes of Freudian motifs and analogies. Derrida's reading of Freud ('Freud and the Scene of Writing', in Derrida 1978, pp. 196–231) is yet another parable of deconstruction, a reading aimed at eliciting the metaphors of writing and psychic 'inscription' to which Freud resorts at crucial points of explanation. The upshot is to show that these 'metaphors' are in fact nothing of the kind. Though Freud always uses them by way of analogy or descriptive convenience, they become so enmeshed in his texts as to offer the most cogent and finally *inescapable* account of unconscious working. 'Physical content will be represented by a text whose essence is irreducibly graphic' (ibid., p. 199). When Freud envisages the unconscious as in some sense structured like a language, his terms of description are borrowed from the economy of *writing* rather than of speech. As Derrida shows, the entire Freudian topology of unconscious meaning depends on such notions as 'trace', 'spacing', 'difference' and others whose place can be found only within a graphic system of representation. Freud held to the belief that these were merely metaphors pointing toward a mature neurological science which would finally dispense with such figurative props. Derrida argues, on the contrary, that Freud's indelible figures of writing are his chief contribution to a knowledge of the unconscious and its effects, in comparison with which his 'neurological fable' must itself be seen as a species of sublimated metaphor. Freud thus stands, with Husserl and Saussure, as a thinker whose texts uphold the tradition of Western metaphysics, yet which yield – through a deconstructive reading – critical motifs at odds with that tradition. Writing asserts itself despite Freud's will to restrict it to a figural and secondary status. As Derrida predicts, 'it is with a graphematics still to come, rather than with a linguistics dominated by an ancient phonologism, that psychoanalysis sees itself as destined to collaborate' (ibid., p. 220).

Derrida's reading of Freud gives some idea of what Bloom most objects to in the practice of deconstruction. It is a reading that totally discounts the psychic drama, the conflicts of will and motive, which Bloom seizes on by way of analogy with the poet's 'anxiety of influence'. Freud himself is for Bloom one of the master-spirits of modern interpretation, a 'strong' wrestler with unconscious meanings whose pattern he projects into powerful new myths of explanation. If Bloom, like Derrida, has little use for the 'scientific' side of Freudian theory, he is equally opposed to a deconstructive reading that would dissolve psychoanalysis into an undifferentiated play of textual meaning. 'The theoreticians of deconstruction in effect say, "In the beginning was the trope", rather than "In the beginning was the troper"' (Bloom 1977, p. 393). If the concept of trope is in itself a species of metaphor, a 'figure of figures', then it is up to the strong-willed interpreter (poet or critic) to assert the possibility of meaning in an otherwise meaningless chain of reductions. Derrida's Freud is the producer of texts which everywhere reveal their unwitting dependence on a rhetoric that self-deconstructs into tropes and yet further tropes of writing. Bloom's Freud is a strong precursor who resists such readings by the power to convert them to his own imaginative end.

His deconstructing colleagues are by no means blind to the dangers and temptations Bloom perceives. Even Hartman sounds the occasional cautionary note when he contemplates the giddying prospects opened up by a pure rhetoric of tropes and intertextuality. His sense of excitement at the freedoms offered to interpretative style goes along with a certain mistrust of the blurring of distinctions between 'text' and 'commentary' entailed by Derrida's philosophy. The problem is bound up with that move 'beyond formalism' which also dissolves the authority of 'the book'.

> By diminishing the book-centeredness of literary discourse you bring it closer to philosophical discourse and run the risk of homogenizing it. True, you may still have 'texts' rather than 'books' – but what constitutes a text is a slippery thing to define . . .   (Hartman 1975, p. 13)

In Derrida Hartman notes the use of a 'highly repetitive and snippety canon', a habit of mixing text and citation which produces in the end 'a highly frustrating *clair-obscur*'.

Hartman's doubts are not serious enough to prevent him from rising to Derrida's challenge with a consciously Nietzschean swagger and verve. Bloom and de Man, in their different ways, represent a more powerful inward check on the centrifugal energies of deconstruction. Bloom's is a frankly rhetorical summons to arrest and reverse what he sees as a movement of 'serene linguistic nihilism', bent upon endless reductive ploys. His style is embattled and his arguments pitched at a sometimes desperate level of urgent pleading. De Man writes from the opposite standpoint of a critic completely given over to the rigours of deconstruction. He is by far the toughest-minded of those 'conceptual rhetoricians' whose thinking and influence Bloom is at such pains to confront. Yet his readings most often come out, as we have seen, at a point where deconstruction has to acknowledge the 'performative' element, or will to meaning, which eludes its subtlest endeavours. Bloom and de Man can be said to arrive at similar conclusions from radically different premises. They both stand apart from what they see – Bloom quite explicitly, de Man by implication – as a facile misuse of deconstructionist theory.

7
Conclusion:
dissenting voices

Bloom sets up as the opponent from within, meeting the deconstructors point for point on rhetorical ground of their own choos-
ing. He thinks it impossible to answer a thoroughgoing scepticism except by fearlessly taking its measure and then responding
with an equal and opposite will to persuade. Others would see
Bloom's tactics as wholly misconceived, an uncalled-for yielding of hostages where a straightforward offensive is the proper
response. Others again, like Murray Krieger, have tried to coax
deconstruction down by arguing that its 'methods' are not, after
all, so very different from those of the old New Criticism (see
Krieger 1979). Much of this debate has been ephemeral and
fruitless, a virtual repetition of the quarrels that surrounded the
first obtrusions of structuralist thought on the American scene.

On the other hand there have been serious attempts to
grapple with deconstruction on alternative philosophic ground.
These mostly start out from the view that scepticism is *not* (as
even Bloom seems forced to admit) irrefutable on its own terms
of argument. Indeed, it may turn out to be self-refuting if one
asks the sceptic by what special privilege his own arguments are
exempt from doubt or mistrust (see Abrams 1978). The deconstructors clearly expect that their texts will be read with care
and attention, their arguments weighed and their conclusions
discussed in a decently responsible manner. Yet how can this be
squared with their own professed scepticism towards meaning,

logic, truth and the very possibility of communication? Their case might seem open to what the philosopher Jürgen Habermas, in a slightly different context, has called the 'transcendental *tu quoque*'. That is, they demand that their texts be properly understood – or at least intelligently read – while ostensibly denying the power of language to encompass any such end.

These objections have little force against a critic like de Man, whose extreme scepticism paradoxically creates a scrupulous regard for the text he interprets. The approach may be condemned as perverse – a virtual technique for creating obstacles to thought – but it remains closely argued and never gives way to a relativistic free-for-all of meaning. Derrida is likewise too canny a sceptic to be caught with his textual defences down. Even while 'playing old Harry' (as the translation puts it) with Searle's intentions, he can argue that his opponent has ignored *the letter* of his (Derrida's) original text and thus laid himself open to a riddling rejoinder. His disregard for the conventional pieties of interpretation goes along with a meticulous attention to detail and a stubborn insistence on the letter of the text, its refusal to be explained away by any convenient means. Derrida's scepticism is not what some of his interpreters would make of it, a passport to limitless interpretative games of their own happy devising. This applies even to the latest texts in translation where the ideas of free play and intertextuality are pushed to a provocative extreme. The point is that Derrida, unlike some of his disciples, has arrived at this position through a long and strenuous process of deconstruction. It may seem quaintly moralistic to say that he has 'earned' this right by actually *thinking through* the problems his followers have picked up, as it were, ready-made. Yet this was already Derrida's contention in *Of Grammatology*: that thought can break with its delusive prehistory only by constantly and actively rehearsing that break. Otherwise deconstruction remains an ineffectual gesture, a theory confined by the very oppositions it seeks to overthrow. It is here, Derrida warns, 'that the concept and above all the work of deconstruction, its "style", remain by nature exposed to misunderstanding and nonrecognition' (Derrida 1977a, p. 28)

Derrida's is not, in other words, a knock-down scepticism easily arrived at and just as easily refuted by a simple *tu quoque*.

It is a hard-won position sustained by arguments that merit the same close *textual* scrutiny Derrida brings to his own best readings. On the other hand there are opposing views of language, truth and meaning which cannot be dismissed as merely naïve or philosophically bankrupt. Derrida implicitly acknowledges their force in his text on Austin. Deconstruction neither denies nor really affects the commonsense view that language exists to communicate meaning. It *suspends* that view for its own specific purpose of seeing what happens when the writs of convention no longer run.

Scepticism in philosophy has always borne this ambiguous relation to the 'natural' or commonsense attitude. Its proponents have never pretended that life could be conducted in a practical way if everyone acted consistently on sceptical assumptions. What would such 'consistency' amount to, indeed, if one denied the very bases of reason and logical coherence? This is not to say that the sceptics' questions are trivial or totally misconceived. They are – as I have tried to show with Derrida – questions that present themselves *compulsively* as soon as one abandons the commonsense position. But language continues to communicate, as life goes on, despite all the problems thrown up by sceptical thought.

Richard Rorty has stated the issue with fine lucidity in his essay 'Philosophy as a Kind of Writing' (Rorty 1978). There are, he argues, two 'traditions' of philosophy which exist in a state of perpetual rivalry, but which can never properly *confront* one another because their aims and idioms are so remote. On the one hand are those thinkers who rest on the conviction that philosophy is a rational dialogue of minds pursued from age to age in the quest for communicable truth. Scepticism is allowed a place in this philosophy, but only so long as it serves to clear away mystification and establish more firmly the indubitable bases of truth. Opposed to this tradition is another, more disparate company of minds, one that carries out periodic raids and incursions into 'mainstream' philosophy. These thinkers reject the rational consensus and thrive on their energies of paradox and style. Philosophy as 'writing', in Rorty's sense, uses language not as a more or less efficient means of rational exchange but as a fighting-ground on which to conduct its major campaigns. The self-conscious practice of philosophic *style* goes along with a rooted scepticism about ultimate truth and method. These two traditions have grown up through various historical shapes and guises. In current Anglo-American perception the line seems to fall between common-sense reason and the 'continental' strain descending from Hegel, through Nietzsche, to the modern French 'excesses'. From the other side things look very different, as may be gathered from Derrida's quizzical dealings with Austin and Searle.

To see these philosophies as locked in dispute, or as both competing for the same objective, is according to Rorty a misapprehension. Their sporadic skirmishing is really nothing more than the result of chance encounters. The distance between them is expressed by Derrida in his closing reflections on the exchange with Searle:

> I ask myself if we will ever be quits with this confrontation.
> Will it have taken place, this time?
> Quite?   (Derrida 1977c, p. 251)

This sense of non-encounter is what Rorty perceives as the gulf between commonsense-rationalist philosophies and those that drive beyond the limits of plain-speaking reason. 'Writing' is in this sense the symptom and accomplice of a radical linguistic scepticism.

Wittgenstein: language and scepticism

The counter-arguments to deconstruction have therefore been situated mostly on commonsense, or 'ordinary-language' ground. There is support from the philosopher Ludwig Wittgenstein (1889–1951) for the view that such sceptical philosophies of language rest at bottom on a false epistemology, one that seeks (and inevitably fails) to discover some *logical correspondence* between language and the world. Wittgenstein himself started out from such a position, but came round to believing that language had many uses and legitimating 'grammars', none of them reducible to a clear-cut logic of explanatory concepts. His later philosophy repudiates the notion that meaning must entail some one-to-one link or 'picturing' relationship between word and referent. Language is now conceived of as a repertoire of 'games' or enabling conventions, as diverse in nature as the jobs they are required to do (Wittgenstein 1953). The nagging problems of philosophy most often resulted, Wittgenstein thought, from the failure to recognize this multiplicity of language games. Philosophers looked for logical solutions to problems which were only created in the first place by a narrow and self-defeating concept of logic. Scepticism, he argued, was the upshot of a deluded quest for certainty in areas of meaning and interpretation that are resistant to logical account.

Wittgenstein's philosophy of language clearly has its anti-deconstructionist uses. If our ways of talking about the world are a matter of tacit convention, then scepticism is simply beside the point, a misplaced scruple produced by a false epistemology. Wittgenstein sees the history of philosophic thought as both bedevilled and largely sustained by such self-created puzzles. His line of reply is understandably attractive to those who reject deconstruction and seek a philosophy of meaning to put in its place. From a Wittgensteinian viewpoint, there is a basic and persistent error of thought in the post-Saussurian textual theory which makes such a startling phenomenon of the split between 'signifier' and 'signified'. To see this as a problem or paradox is to repeat the traditional mistake, that which comes of expecting language to relate directly to objects or ideas. Such, according to Wittgenstein and his disciples, is the root of all sceptical philosophies. They are driven into bewilderment and paradox by failing to notice the variety of possible 'fits' between language, logic and reality.

This argument would seem to offer an alternative, if not a full-scale rejoinder, to post-structuralist textual theories. The appeal to 'ordinary language', with its implicit sanctions and conventions, is seen as a more sensible way of coming to terms with the arbitrary nature of the sign. Structuralism – it might be argued – is fixated on the age-old delusion which, in one form or another, has always preoccupied philosophy. This gave rise to those attacks on 'realist' fiction (by Barthes among others) which seemed to assume that author and reader were incapable of telling narrative illusion from straight reportage. The rift between sign and referent became a high point of radical theory; it was forgotten that fiction has always been more or less aware of its own fictionality, even if the symptoms were not always there on the surface, as in some post-modernist texts. A Wittgensteinian approach would reject such paradoxical 'readings' (like Barthes's *S/Z*) as based on a perverse and myopic idea of how language actually adapts to the flexible conventions of narrative.

Other objectors have taken a flatly moralistic line. Gerald Graff, for one, has denounced deconstruction as a culpable retreat from the problems of modern society, a kind of textual fiddling while Rome burns (see Graff 1979). Graff thinks that the new rhetoricians have much more in common with the 'old' New Criticism than they like to believe. What both movements come down to, he argues, is a form of sophisticated escapism, denying literature any power to engage with 'real' experience. Where modernism had started out (with Eliot, Joyce and their contemporaries) as a genuine protest against the reductive monopoly of old-style realist convention, it has now taken hold as a kind of institutional escape-route, totally divorced from any sense of social engagement.

Graff sees the same debilitating influence at work in the 'post-modernist' style of fiction practised by writers like Thomas Pynchon and Donald Barthelme. If realism is merely a matter of dominant convention, with no more claims to truth than other, more self-conscious modes of writing, then the way is clearly open to a wholesale scepticism which acknowledges only the infinite play of textual inscription. The trouble with Graff's toughminded stance is that it doesn't engage with his opponents in any real argumentative way. He lumps them all together, critics and novelists alike, as self-condemned enemies of reason, without seeing – or allowing himself to see – the force of their case. Thus Frank Kermode is taken to task for his argument (in *The Sense of an Ending*) that we always interpret texts in humanly satisfying ways, despite our awareness that such meanings are tentative and provisional, not to be confused with practical truths. Graff treats this as yet another case of last-ditch critical manoeuvring, a desperate attempt to reclaim vital ground which should never have been yielded in the first place. Yet Graff himself argues to much the same effect as Kermode when he appeals to Wittgenstein on the communal sense-making role of *conventions* in language and fiction. His appeal is more assertive than Kermode's – not so much hedged about with qualifications – but presents a similar tactical line of defence.

Wittgenstein is always at hand with a knock-down argument against thoroughgoing scepticism: that 'if you tried to doubt everything you would not get as far as doubting anything. The game of doubting itself presupposes certainty' (quoted by Graff 1979, p. 195). But this, once again, is to throw the whole argument back on to a bedrock of flatly commonsense assertion which hardly meets the deconstructionist challenge. There is a dead-end to Graff's line of argument where he simply ignores – rather than thinking through – the issues raised by deconstruction. His mistake is to believe that these problems can be neatly cleared away by tracing them back, explaining where they came from historically and why they have continued to exert such an influence. In this case, according to Graff, the line can be followed via the New Critics to Kant and his Romantic descendants, with their puzzling over mind and its relation to 'objective' reality. But the puzzles remain, and indeed provide critics like de Man with a rich prehistory for their deconstructive arguments.

It is the same with Graff's halfway redemptive readings of post-modernist novelists like Pynchon and Barthelme. On the one hand, Graff condemns their lack of intellectual fight in (supposedly) endorsing the hopelessness, 'anomie' and defeatist scepticism of modern society. On the other, he wants to wrench them away from this collective despair by offering hints of an alternative, 'adversary' reading. Thus Barthelme's stories 'call attention to their own inability to overcome their imprisonment in the artifices of language and the solipsism of consciousness, though it should not be forgotten that this very strategy itself makes a statement' (Graff 1979, pp. 236–7). Well, one or the other, but surely not both, unless – as Graff seems otherwise unwilling to admit – the 'meaning' of a text is open to all manner of strategic (mis)interpretations. Here, as with his anti-deconstructivist thrusts, Graff seems to offer not so much a worked-out critique as a kind of desperate moral imperative, eloquently stated but nowhere argued beyond a sticking-point of commonsense assumption.

There is more force to the argument from Wittgenstein when applied to some of the recent, stereotyped versions of deconstructive theory. A glance at the current American journals will show how deconstruction has taken hold, not only in new publications like *Glyph* and *Diacritics* but even in the august pages of *PMLA*. The rate of production is such that all the canonical poems and novels will soon have a deconstructionist 'reading', to place alongside the New Critical, Marxist and other competing approaches. Abrams views this proliferating output – not without reason – as a sign that deconstruction is falling prey to mere ingenuity and academic oneupmanship.

The truth is that deconstructionist theory can only be as useful and enlightening as the mind that puts it to work. Some current applications, especially in the field of narrative analysis, do bear the marks of a certain routine ingenuity. They mostly take the form of paradoxical 'double readings', intended to show how novels display their own artifice even when exploiting the realist mode. The peculiar logic of narrative is such that 'effects' are no longer related to 'causes' in a straightforward sequence of unfolding events. Rather, it is the nature of fictional form – the demands of plot and construction – which operate a kind of logical reversal, an affront to commonsense reason. 'Causes' in the novel are brought into play by the need for some solution or (apparently) antecedent fact which explains and unravels a complicated plot. In this sense causes are really *effects*, since they spring from a given complex of events which creates them, as it were, in pursuit of its own coherence. Effects are likewise transformed into causes by the same curious twist of logic (see Jonathan Culler, 'Story and Discourse in the Analysis of Narrative', in Culler 1981, pp. 169–87).

George Eliot's *Daniel Deronda* is a favoured example, inviting such treatment for several reasons. First, it stages a virtual confrontation between the realist mode of the 'Gwendolen Harleth' chapters (the parts Leavis signally approved of) and the visionary strain of the mysteries surrounding Deronda's Jewish identity and sense of mission. From this point of view it can be said to 'deconstruct' the commonsense assumptions linking the ideology of nineteenth-century realism to the judgements of modern conservative critics like Leavis. Moreover, it throws into sharp relief the paradoxes about cause-and-effect which deconstruction is resolved to uncover. The novel represents Deronda as finding out the truth of his racial origin through a series of episodes and 'chance' encounters which seem to point back to some mysterious pre-existent meaning. But the absent 'cause' is itself brought about, in narratological terms, by the events and portents it ultimately serves to explain. Cynthia Chase has hit upon a letter in the novel (from Hans Meyrick to Deronda) which underlines the paradox rather neatly. 'Here at home', he writes,

> the most judicious opinion going as to the effects of present causes is that 'time will show'. As to the present causes of past effects, it is now seen that the late swindling telegrams account for the last year's cattle plague – which is a refutation of philosophy falsely so called, and justifies the compensation to the farmers.   (quoted by Chase 1978, p. 225)

On the face of it a sample of Meyrick's puckish humour, the passage clearly lends itself to deconstructive reading. That effects should 'cause' causes, and causes be constructed as 'effects' of effects, is a Nietzschean paradox that runs nicely athwart the logic of convention.

But these ideas about narrative, though strikingly formulated, are after all not so remarkable. That novels are *constructed* in a certain way – and to that extent reorder the 'logic' of contingent events – is known upon a moment's reflection to every reader. The corollary that the two narrative 'logics' are inherently at odds is by no means so obvious, and it suggests a certain effort to seek out self-supporting puzzles and paradoxes. In fact it amounts to what philosophers would call a 'category mistake', a confusion of logical realms or orders of discourse. Structuralist theory was clear enough about the basic distinction between 'story' and 'plot', the one an implied (and imaginably real-life) sequence of events, the other a pattern imposed by the requirements of narrative form. They represent two different kinds of reading: the latter is attentive to structure and device, while the former rests on a willing – but not necessarily naïve – suspension of disbelief. To see them as locked in conflict or paradox is to mistake the conventions of narrative for the rigours of logical discourse. The tactics of 'double-reading' automatically generate the kind of paradoxical impasse they set out to find. Like the structuralist attack on that ubiquitous chimera the 'classic realist text', such strategies ignore the variety of possible relations between language, text and reality.

But this is deconstruction in a facile guise far removed from the vigour and sheer argumentative power of Derrida or de Man at their best. Of course it is too early as yet to predict what effects deconstruction will have on the wider practice of critical and philosophic writing. For de Man the deconstructive opening is a summons not to be ignored: criticism, he says, will have its work cut out for years to come, that is if it wishes to measure its strength against this new and rigorous textual awareness. Others may dismiss such claims or view them with frank alarm. What is clear already is that critics very largely out of sympathy with deconstruction have registered its impact and felt the need to argue their case with circumspect care. Denis Donoghue, for one, has taken issue with Derrida in his book *The Sovereign Ghost* (1976). Donoghue comes out, as one might expect, for the saving power of poetic presence – or 'imagination' – as against Derrida's determined assault on such notions. Murray Krieger likewise, as a rearguard defender of the old New Criticism, challenges Derrida on the grounds that poetry, at least, partakes of a vitalizing presence that eludes the abysmal textuality of tropes (Krieger 1979).

Neither of these is an 'answer' to Derrida, in the sense of posing an obstacle to the activity of thought and the process of displacement that deconstruction has set in train. Both, on the other hand, bear witness to the unsettling power of Derrida's texts. Deconstruction has marked out a new domain of argument for the age-old quarrel between 'literature' and 'philosophy'. The claims of analysis have never been pressed so far as by conceptual rhetoricians like de Man. Nor has criticism ever taken on such courage, intellectual and stylistic, in asserting its claim as a self-respecting discipline of thought. To ignore that claim is to close one's mind to something other, and more, than a short-lived swing of critical fashion.

References

Abrams, M. H. (1978) 'How To Do Things With Texts'. *Partisan Review*, XLIV, 566–88.

Austin, J. L. (1963) *How To Do Things With Words*. London: Oxford University Press.

Barthes, Roland (1967) *Elements of Semiology*. Trans. Annette Lavers and Colin Smith. London: Jonathan Cape.

Barthes, Roland (1975) *S/Z*. Trans. Richard Miller. London: Jonathan Cape.

Barthes, Roland (1977) *Roland Barthes by Roland Barthes*. Trans. Richard Howard. London: Macmillan.

Barthes, Roland (1979) *A Lover's Discourse*. Trans. Richard Howard. London: Jonathan Cape.

Belsey, Catherine (1980) *Critical Practice*. London: Methuen.

Blackmur, R. P. (1967) *A Primer of Ignorance*. New York: Harcourt Brace.

Bloom, Harold (1959) *Shelley's Mythmaking*. New Haven, Conn.: Yale University Press.

Bloom, Harold (1973) *The Anxiety of Influence: A Theory of Poetry*. New York and London: Oxford University Press.

Bloom, Harold (1975) *Kabbalah and Criticism*. New York: Seabury Press.

Bloom, Harold (1976) *Poetry and Repression*. New Haven, Conn.: Yale University Press.

Bloom, Harold (1977) *Wallace Stevens: The Poems of Our Climate*. Ithaca, NY, and London: Cornell University Press.

Chase, Cynthia (1978) 'The Decomposition of the Elephants: Double-Reading *Daniel Deronda*'. *PMLA* XCIII, 215–27.

Cornford, F. M. (1932) *Before and After Socrates*. Cambridge: Cambridge University Press.

Culler, Jonathan (1972) 'Frontiers of Criticism' (review of Paul de Man's *Blindness and Insight*). *The Yale Review* (Winter 1972), 259–71.

Culler, Jonathan (1975) *Structuralist Poetics*. London: Routledge & Kegan Paul.

Culler, Jonathan (1981) *The Pursuit of Signs: Semiotics, Literature, Deconstruction*. London: Routledge & Kegan Paul.

de Man, Paul (1969) 'The Rhetoric of Temporality'. In Charles S. Singleton (ed.), *Interpretation: Theory and Practice*. Baltimore, Md: Johns Hopkins University Press.

de Man, Paul (1971) *Blindness and Insight: Essays in the Rhetoric of Contemporary Criticism*. London and New York: Oxford University Press.

de Man, Paul (1979) *Allegories of Reading: Figural Language in Rousseau, Nietzsche, Rilke, and Proust*. New Haven, Conn.: Yale University Press.

Derrida, Jacques (1972a) *La Dissémination*. Paris: Seuil.

Derrida, Jacques (1972b) *Marges de la philosophie*. Paris: Minuit.

Derrida, Jacques (1973) *Speech and Phenomena, and Other Essays on Husserl's Theory of Signs*. Trans. David B. Allison. Evanston Ill.: Northwestern University Press.

Derrida, Jacques (1974a) *Glas*. Paris: Galilée.

Derrida, Jacques (1974b) 'The White Mythology: Metaphor in the Text of Philosophy'. *New Literary History*, VI, 1, 7–74.

Derrida, Jacques (1977a) *Of Grammatology*. Trans. Gayatri Chakravorty Spivak. Baltimore, Md: Johns Hopkins University Press.

Derrida, Jacques (1977b) 'Signature Event Context'. *Glyph*, I, 172–97.

Derrida, Jacques (1977c) 'Limited Inc. abc'. *Glyph*, II, 162–254.

Derrida, Jacques (1978) *Writing and Difference*. Trans. Alan Bass. London: Routledge & Kegan Paul.

Derrida, Jacques (1979) *Spurs: Nietzsche's Styles*. Trans. Barbara Harlow. Chicago, Ill.: Chicago University Press.

Derrida, Jacques (1981) *Positions*. Trans. Alan Bass. London: Athlone Press.

Donoghue, Denis (1976) *The Sovereign Ghost: Studies in Imagination*. Berkeley, Calif.: University of California Press.

Eagleton, Terry (1976) *Criticism and Ideology*. London: New Left Books.

Empson, William (1961) *Seven Types of Ambiguity*. 2nd edn. Harmondsworth: Penguin.

Foucault, Michel (1977) *Language, Counter-Memory, Practice*. Trans. Donald F. Bouchard and Sherry Simon. Oxford: Blackwell.

Graff, Gerald (1979) *Literature Against Itself: Literary Ideas in Modern Society*. Chicago, Ill., and London: University of Chicago Press.

Hartman, Geoffrey (1970) *Beyond Formalism*. New Haven, Conn., and London: Yale University Press.

Hartman, Geoffrey (1975) *The Fate of Reading and Other Essays*. Chicago, Ill., and London: University of Chicago Press.

Hartman, Geoffrey (1978) 'The Recognition Scene of Criticism'. *Critical Inquiry*, IV, 407–16.

Hartman, Geoffrey (ed.) (1979) *Deconstruction and Criticism*. London: Routledge & Kegan Paul.

Hartman, Geoffrey (1980) *Criticism in the Wilderness*. New Haven, Conn., and London: Yale University Press.

Hawkes, Terence (1977) *Structuralism and Semiotics*. London: Methuen.

Husserl, Edmund (1964) *The Phenomenology of Internal Time-Consciousness*. Trans. James S. Churchill. Bloomington, Ind.: Indiana University Press.

Husserl, Edmund (1970) *The Crisis of European Sciences and Transcendental Phenomenology*. Trans. David Carr. Evanston, Ill.: Northwestern University Press.

Jameson, Frederic (1971) *Marxism and Form*. Princeton, NJ: Princeton University Press.

Jameson, Frederic (1972) *The Prison-House of Language*. Princeton, NJ: Princeton University Press.

Krieger, Murray (1979) *Poetic Presence and Illusion*. Baltimore, Md, and London: Johns Hopkins University Press.

Leavis, F. R. (1937) 'Literary Criticism and Philosophy' (reply to Rene Wellek). *Scrutiny*, VI, 59–70.

Lentricchia, Frank (1980) *After the New Criticism*. London: Athlone Press.

Lévi-Strauss, Claude (1961) *Tristes Tropiques*. Trans. John Russell. London: Hutchinson.

Lévi-Strauss, Claude (1966) *The Savage Mind*. London: Weidenfeld & Nicolson.

Lodge, David (1977) *The Modes of Modern Writing: Metaphor, Metonymy, and the Typology of Modern Literature*. London: Edward Arnold.

Macherey, Pierre (1978) *A Theory of Literary Production*. Trans. Geoffrey Wall. London: Routledge & Kegan Paul.

Marx, Karl (1968) 'The Eighteenth Brumaire of Louis Bonaparte'. In *Marx and Engels: Selected Works*, 96–179. London: Lawrence & Wishart.

Mehlman, Jeffrey (1979) *Revolution and Repetition*. Berkeley & Los Angeles, Calif.: University of California Press.

Merleau-Ponty, Maurice (1962) *The Phenomenology of Perception*. London: Routledge & Kegan Paul.

Merleau-Ponty, Maurice (1964) *Signs*. Trans. McCleary. Evanston, Ill.: Northwestern University Press.

Miller, J. Hillis (1966) 'The Geneva School'. *The Critical Quarterly*, VIII, 305–21.

Miller, J. Hillis (1970) *Thomas Hardy: Distance and Desire*. Cambridge, Mass.: Harvard University Press.

Miller, J. Hillis (1977) 'The Limits of Pluralism, II: The Critic as Host'. *Critical Inquiry*, III, 439–47.

Nietzsche, Friedrich (1954) *The Portable Nietzsche*. Trans. and ed. Walter Kaufmann. New York: Viking.

Nietzsche, Friedrich (1977) *A Nietzsche Reader*. Selected and trans. R. J. Hollingdale. Harmondsworth: Penguin.

Ong, Walter J. (1962) *The Barbarian Within*. New York: Macmillan.

Plato (1960) *The Gorgias*. Intro. and trans. Walter Hamilton. Harmondsworth: Penguin.

Plato (1973) *The Phaedrus and Letters VII and VIII*. Intro. and trans. Walter Hamilton. Harmondsworth: Penguin.

Pirsig, Robert M. (1974) *Zen and the Art of Motorcycle Maintenance*. London: The Bodley Head.

Richards, I. A. (1924) *Principles of Literary Criticism*. London: Paul Trench Trubner.

Richards, I. A. (1936) *The Philosophy of Rhetoric*. London and New York: Oxford University Press.

Rorty, Richard (1978) 'Philosophy as a Kind of Writing'. *New Literary History*, X, 141–60.

Russell, Bertrand (1954) *A History of Western Philosophy*. London: Allen & Unwin.

Said, Edward (1978) *Orientalism*. New York: Pantheon.

Said, Edward (1979) 'The Text, the World, the Critic'. In Josué V. Harari (ed.), *Textual Strategies: Perspectives in Post-Structuralist Criticism*, 161–88. London: Methuen.

Saussure, Ferdinand de (1974) *Course in General Linguistics*. Trans. Wade Baskin. London: Fontana.

Searle, John R. (1972) *Speech Acts: An Essay in the Philosophy of Language*. Cambridge: Cambridge University Press.

Searle, John R. (1977) 'Reiterating the Differences' (reply to Derrida). *Glyph*, I, 198–208.

Tate, Allen (1953) *The Forlorn Demon*. Chicago, Ill.: Regnery.

Thody, Philip (1977) *Roland Barthes: A Conservative Estimate*. London: Macmillan.

Wimsatt, William K. (1954) *The Verbal Icon: Studies in the Meaning of Poetry*. Lexington, Ky: University of Kentucky Press.

Wimsatt, William K. (1970) 'Battering the Object: The Ontological Approach'. In Bradbury and Palmer (eds), *Contemporary Criticism*. London: Edward Arnold.

Wittgenstein, Ludwig (1953) *Philosophical Investigations*. Trans. G. E. M. Anscombe. Oxford: Blackwell.

Notes for further reading

These notes are intended to supplement the References section, where the reader will find full details of works referred to in the text. For obvious space-saving reasons I have avoided duplicating entries, except in the case of Derrida and other primary sources (de Man, Hartman, etc.) whose omission would create an oddly lopsided effect. Needless to say this is a highly selective listing, a series of signposts the reader can follow up to a point before branching off into regions of his or her own special interest. Items are arranged under two main headings: (1) Derrida, (2) Deconstruction in America, the latter ranging more widely over various post-structuralist debates.

Derrida

Texts in English translation

Speech and Phenomena, and Other Essays on Husserl's Theory of Signs. Trans. David B. Allison. Evanston, Ill.: Northwestern University Press, 1973. First published in French 1967. (See above, Chapter 3.)

'The White Mythology: Metaphor in the Text of Philosophy. *New Literary History*, VI, 1 (1974), 7–74.

Of Grammatology. Trans. Gayatri Chakravorty Spivak. Baltimore, Md: Johns Hopkins University Press, 1977. First published in French 1967. Contains lengthy but accessible discussions of Rousseau, Saussure, Lévi-Strauss and the problematic status of writing in Western tradition. Together with the detailed Translator's Preface, these texts make up the best introduction to Derrida's thought.

'Signature Event Context'. *Glyph,* I (1977), 172–97. This deconstruction of speech-act philosophy was followed up by John Searle's
rejoinder, 'Reiterating the Differences', *Glyph,* 1 (1977), 198–208.
The exchange was capped by Derrida, 'Limited Inc abc', *Glyph,* II
(1977), 162–254.

Edmund Husserl's Origin of Geometry. Trans. Edward Leavey. Stony-
brook: Hays, 1978. First published in French 1962. Argues that
writing and its structures of *differance* are always already presupposed, even by the 'ideal' truths of mathematics. A difficult and
specialized text, though closely related to *Speech and Phenomena.*

Writing and Difference. Trans. Alan Bass. London: Routledge & Kegan
Paul, 1978. First published in French 1967. Contains, among other
things, important essays on Hegel, Freud, Foucault and Lévi-
Strauss. Also the most explicit of Derrida's reflections on structuralism and its discontents. Should be read as a sequel to *Of Grammatology,* though the essays were written during the same period and
share many themes.

'Speculations – on Freud'. Trans. Ian McLeod. *The Oxford Literary
Review,* III, 2 (1978), 78–97. Continues the deconstructive treatment
of psychoanalysis taken up in 'Freud and the Scene of Writing' (in
Writing and Difference).

Spurs: Nietzsche's Styles. Trans. Barbara Harlow. Chicago, Ill.: Chicago
University Press, 1979. Parallel texts in French and English. Derrida
at his most elusive and extravagant, shuttling from Heidegger to Nietzsche's umbrella and the 'question of woman' in
philosophy. Best approached via the pages on Nietzsche in *Writing
and Difference.*

'Living On'. In Geoffrey Hartman (ed.), *Deconstruction and Criticism.*
London: Routledge & Kegan Paul, 1979. Derrida's contribution to
the Yale critics' symposium, ostensibly focusing (like the others) on
Shelley's poem 'The Triumph of Life', but soon launching out on to
speculative paths of its own. Very much a case of deconstruction 'on
the wild side'.

'The Supplement of Copula: Philosophy *before* Linguistics'. In Josué V.
Harari (ed.), *Textual Strategies: Perspectives in Post-Structuralist Criticism.* London: Methuen, 1979. Deconstructs the 'grammar' of Western philosophy (Aristotle to Heidegger), as determined by the
predicative structure of language. A difficult but important text.

Positions. Trans. Alan Bass. London: Athlone Press, 1981. First published in French 1972. Contains the texts of Derrida's interviews
with Henri Ronse, Julia Kristeva, Jean-Louis Houdebine and Guy
Scarpetta. Not a handy short-cut to Derrida's ideas but an interesting gloss on some of their implications. The first interview (with
Ronse) is the most accessible and lucid, while the third (Houdebine

and Scarpetta) raises the thorny question of Derrida's attitude to Marxist textual theory.

Texts in French

La Dissémination. Paris: Seuil, 1972. Includes important essays on Plato, Mallarmé and Philippe Sollers. 'La Pharmacie de Platon' is especially crucial for Derrida's account of Greek philosophy and its ambiguously hostile attitude to writing. An English translation is forthcoming from Chicago University Press.

Marges de la philosophie. Paris: Minuit, 1972. Essays on language, philosophy and writing, including the originals of 'The White Mythology' and 'The Supplement of Copula' (see above). A complete translation is currently being prepared for Harvard University Press.

Glas. Paris: Galilée, 1974. Derrida's most graphic demonstration of how texts can invade each other's space and play havoc with the logic of meaning. Hegel and Genet are brought face to face in a kind of perverse interlinear gloss which exposes philosophic reason to the lures and obsessions of a homosexual thief-turned-writer. Through a barrage of puns and typographical devices Hegel's language is wrenched out of context and transformed into a mind-bending parody of itself. *Glas* is an endlessly fascinating text, though its brilliant wordplay will seem little more than that to a reader unfamiliar with Derrida's work. An English translation (if the word is appropriate) is under way.

La Vérité en peinture. Paris: Flammarion, 1978. Deconstructs the notions of expressiveness, truth and authenticity, as presupposed by most art criticism and aesthetics generally. Brings out the affinity between Derrida's thinking and certain ideas of the German-Jewish critic Walter Benjamin, especially his theme of the modern disappearance of cultural 'aura' in an age of mass-produced art.

La Carte postale de Socrate à Freud et au-delà. Paris: Aubier-Flammarion, 1980. Essays on Freud and Lacan, prefaced by a sequence of 'postcards' addressed not to anyone in particular but to the general proposition that 'truth' is a shuttling and homeless exchange of messages, a writing bereft of source or destination. Teasingly contests Lacan's claims for psychoanalysis as the ultimate truth of language, a debate taken up in Derrida's rereading of Poe's 'The Purloined Letter' (a *locus classicus* of Lacanian theory). Plato's 'letters' – which may be apocryphal – become the jumping-off point for Derrida's reflections on the 'forgery' of writing, its limitless capacity for doubt and deception.

Writings on Derrida

The following is necessarily a selective listing of the more important books and articles that have appeared up to 1981. The aim is to represent as many sides as possible of a debate which has often polarized opinion, so that some of these pieces are distinctly hostile to Derrida, while others attempt a variety of mediating stances. Readers in search of more detailed documentation may wish to consult John Leavey and David B. Allison, 'A Derrida Bibliography', *Research in Phenomenology*, VIII (1978), 145–60. This covers Derrida's writings (including those in English translation) up to early 1978, along with more than 200 secondary items, many of them marginal but showing the extraordinary range and resonance of Derrida's impact.

Allison, David B. 'Derrida and Wittgenstein: Playing the Game'. *Research in Phenomenology*, VIII (1978), 93–109.

Altieri, Charles. 'Wittgenstein on Consciousness and Language: A Challenge to Derridean Theory'. *Modern Language Notes*, XCI (1976), 1397–423. (See above, Chapter 7.)

Bass, Alan. ' "Literature"/Literature'. In Richard Macksey (ed.), *Velocities of Change*. Baltimore, Md, and London: Johns Hopkins University Press, 1974, 341–53.

Berezdivin, Ruben. 'Gloves Inside-Out'. *Research in Phenomenology*, VIII (1978), 111–26. Mainly on Derrida's *Glas*.

Brown, P. L. 'Epistemology and Method: Althusser, Foucault, Derrida'. *Research in Phenomenology*, VIII (1978), 147–62.

Cousins, Mark. 'The Logic of Deconstruction'. *The Oxford Literary Review*, III (1978), 70–7.

Culler, Jonathan. 'Jacques Derrida'. In *Structuralism and Since: From Lévi-Strauss to Derrida*, 154–80. London: Oxford University Press, 1979.

Culler, Jonathan. *On Deconstruction*. London: Routledge & Kegan Paul (forthcoming).

Cumming, Robert Denoon. 'The Odd Couple: Heidegger and Derrida'. *Review of Metaphysics*, XXXIV (1981), 487–521.

de Man, Paul. *Blindness and Insight: Essays in the Rhetoric of Contemporary Criticism*. New York and London: Oxford University Press, 1971. Among the earliest American texts to register the impact of deconstruction; contains de Man's intricate critique of Derrida on Rousseau.

Ellman, Maud. 'Spacing Out: A Double Entendre on Mallarmé'. *The Oxford Literary Review*, III (1978), 22–31.

Garver, Newton. Preface to the English translation of Derrida's *Speech and Phenomena*, IX–XXIX. Evanston, Ill.: Northwestern University

Press, 1973. Interesting on the relationship between Derrida's and Wittgenstein's philosophies of language.

Garver, Newton. 'Derrida on Rousseau on Writing'. *Journal of Philosophy*, LXXIV (1977), 663–73.

Grene, Marjorie. 'Life, Death and Language: Some Thoughts on Derrida and Wittgenstein'. In *Philosophy In and Out of Europe*, 142–54. Berkeley and Los Angeles, Calif.: University of California Press, 1976.

Hartman, Geoffrey. 'Monsieur Texte: On Jacques Derrida, His *Glas*' and 'Monsieur Texte II: Epiphany in Echoland'. *Georgia Review*, XXIX, 4, and XXX, 1 (1975–6).

Hartman, Geoffrey. 'Crossing Over: Literary Commentary as Literature'. *Comparative Literature*, XXVIII (1976), 257–76. Takes Derrida's *Glas* as a pretext for Hartman's critical-liberationist plea.

Hartman, Geoffrey. *Saving the Text: Literature/Derrida/Philosophy*. Baltimore, Md: Johns Hopkins University Press, 1981.

Hoy, David Couzens. *The Critical Circle: Literature and History in Contemporary Hermeneutics*. Berkeley and Los Angeles, Calif.: University of California Press, 1978. Useful chapter on Derrida's differences with Heidegger, Gadamer and current hermeneutics.

Johnson, Barbara. 'The Frame of Reference: Poe, Lacan, Derrida'. *Literature and Psychoanalysis, Yale French Studies*, 55–6 (1977), 457–505.

La Capra, Dominick. 'Habermas and the Grounding of Critical Theory'. *History and Theory*, XVI (1977), 237–64. Compares the relation between textual theory and historical understanding in Derrida, Foucault and representatives of the Frankfurt School.

McDonald, C. V. 'Jacques Derrida's Reading of Rousseau'. *The Eighteenth Century* (Texas), XX (1979), 82–95.

Mulligan, Kevin. 'Inscriptions and Speaking's Place: Derrida and Wittgenstein'. *The Oxford Literary Review*, VIII (1978), 62–7.

Norris, Christopher. 'Jacques Derrida's Grammatology'. *Poetry Nation Review*, VI, 2 (1978), 38–40.

Norris, Christopher. 'The Margins of Meaning: Derrida's *Spurs*'. *The Cambridge Quarterly*, IX, 3 (1980), 280–4.

Norris, Christopher. 'The Polymetaphorical Mailman' (review of Derrida's *La Carte postale de Socrate à Freud*). *The Times Literary Supplement*, 4 July 1980, 761.

Ricœur, Paul. *The Rule of Metaphor*. London: Routledge & Kegan Paul, 1978. Argues from a broadly 'hermeneutic' viewpoint not wholly sympathetic to deconstruction, but contains some interesting pages on Derrida's essay 'The White Mythology'.

Rorty, Richard. 'Derrida on Language, Being and Abnormal Philosophy'. *Journal of Philosophy*, LXXIV (1977), 673–81.

Rorty, Richard. 'Philosophy as a Kind of Writing'. *New Literary History*,

X' (1978), 141–60. A lively account of Derrida's differences with 'normal' (i.e. consensual and rationalist) modes of philosophizing.

Said, Edward. 'The Problem of Textuality: Two Exemplary Positions'. *Critical Inquiry*, IV (1978), 673–714. Contrasts Derrida's textual hermeticism ('il n'y a pas de hors-texte') with Foucault's commitment to an activating rhetoric of 'worldly' discursive practices.

Silverman, Hugh J. 'Self-Decentering: Derrida Incorporated'. *Research in Phenomenology*, VIII (1978), 45–65. On Derrida's deconstruction of the transcendental ego, or self-possessed subject of traditional psychology.

Ulmer, J. L. 'Jacques Derrida and Paul de Man on/in Rousseau's Faults'. *The Eighteenth Century* (Texas), XX (1979), 164–81.

Woods D. C. 'An Introduction to Derrida'. *Radical Philosophy*, 21 (1979), 18–28. Combines lucid exposition with critique from a Marxist-activist viewpoint.

Wordsworth, Ann. 'Derrida and Criticism'. *The Oxford Literary Review*, III (1978), 47–52.

Deconstruction in America

This section is mainly concerned with Bloom, de Man, Hartman and Miller, along with those critics who have attacked their position or entered the debate with something important to say. I have not given details of 'pre-deconstructionist' texts by the Yale critics, except (as in Hartman's case) where they offer a kind of exemplary progress through and beyond the 'old' New Criticism.

Abrams, M. H. 'How To Do Things With Texts'. *Partisan Review*, XLIV (1978), 566–88. Charges the deconstructors with practising a double and deceptive strategy: denying that language can possess any definite, communicable sense, while expecting their own texts to be carefully and properly interpreted. By no means a knock-down argument – as witness Derrida versus Searle – but a salutary riposte to deconstruction in its less circumspect forms. See also:

Abrams, M. H. 'The Limits of Pluralism: The Deconstructive Angel'. *Critical Inquiry*, III (1977), 425–38.

Altieri, Charles. 'Presence and Reference in a Literary Text: The Example of Williams' "This Is Just To Say"'. *Critical Inquiry*, V (1979), 489–510. Argues that poetry can establish its own kind of 'presence', momentarily immune to the pure *differance* of writing. Not so much a refutation of Derridean theory as a willing act of faith on the critic's part.

Bloom, Harold. *The Anxiety of Influence: A Theory of Poetry*. New York and

London: Oxford University Press, 1973. (See above, Chapter 6, on Bloom.)

Bloom, Harold. *A Map of Misreading*. New York and London: Oxford University Press, 1975.

Bloom, Harold. *Poetry and Repression*. New Haven, Conn.: Yale University Press, 1976.

Bloom, Harold. *Wallace Stevens: The Poems of Our Climate*. Ithaca, NY: Cornell University Press, 1977. Contains Bloom's most explicit and hard-pressed arguments against deconstruction in its radically textual form.

Chase, Cynthia. 'Oedipal Textuality: Reading Freud's Reading of *Oedipus*'. *Diacritics*, IX (1979), 54–71.

Culler, Jonathan. *Structuralist Poetics*. London: Routledge & Kegan Paul, 1975. Basically a pre-deconstructionist treatment of structuralist theory, with distinct reservations (in the final chapter) about Derrida's then looming influence.

Culler, Jonathan. *The Pursuit of Signs*. London: Routledge & Kegan Paul, 1981. Far more sympathetic toward deconstruction, though treats it as in many ways a geared-up version of the programme announced in *Structuralist Poetics*. Essays on narrative, metaphor, genre theory, etc., showing how thought continually runs up against 'unthinkable' twists of paradox.

Culler, Jonathan. *On Deconstruction*. London: Routledge & Kegan Paul (forthcoming).

de Man, Paul. 'The Rhetoric of Temporality'. In Charles S. Singleton (ed.), *Interpretation: Theory and Practice*, 173–209. Baltimore, Md: Johns Hopkins University Press, 1969. Deconstructs the Romantic ideology of symbol, showing how its meanings break down into the discrete, serial structures of allegory. A brilliant essay; de Man at his most persuasive.

de Man, Paul. 'The Epistemology of Metaphor'. *Critical Inquiry*, V (1978), 13–30. On metaphor in the text of philosophy, with reference mainly to Locke and Kant. Should be read in conjunction with Derrida's 'White Mythology' (see above).

de Man, Paul. *Allegories of Reading: Figural Language in Rousseau Nietzsche, Rilke, and Proust*. New Haven, Conn.: Yale University Press, 1979. (See above, Chapter 6, for a detailed account of this sweepingly ambitious and controversial text.)

de Man, Paul. 'Autobiography as Defacement'. *Modern Language Notes*, XCIV (1979), 918–38.

Felman, Shoshana. 'Turning the Screw of Interpretation'. *Yale French Studies*, 55–6 (1977), 94–207.

Graff, Gerald. *Literature Against Itself: Literary Ideas in Modern Society*. Chicago, Ill., and London: University of Chicago Press, 1979. A polemical attack not only on deconstruction but on post-modern literature and any way of thinking which tries to drive a wedge between the text and 'reality'. Comes down to a mixture of moral indignation and flatly commonsense assertion.

Hartman, Geoffrey. *Beyond Formalism*. New Haven, Conn., and London: Yale University Press, 1970. (Discussed at length in Chapters 1 and 4.)

Hartman, Geoffrey. *The Fate of Reading and Other Essays*. Chicago, Ill., and London: University of Chicago Press, 1975.

Hartman, Geoffrey. 'The Recognition Scene of Criticism'. *Critical Inquiry*, IV (1978), 407–16.

Hartman, Geoffrey (ed.). *Deconstruction and Criticism*. London: Routledge & Kegan Paul, 1979.

Hartman, Geoffrey. *Criticism in the Wilderness*. New Haven, Conn., and London: Yale University Press, 1980. Argues for a newly adventurous 'hermeneutic' criticism aware of its own stylistic resources and open to the liberating influence of thinkers like Derrida, Heidegger and Walter Benjamin.

Jacobs, Carol. *The Dissimulating Harmony: Images of Interpretation in Nietzsche, Rilke and Benjamin*. Baltimore, Md: Johns Hopkins University Press, 1978. Follows de Man in deconstructing the metaphors and tropes that produce the illusion of straightforward textual readability. Suggestive but wayward in argument.

Jacobs, Carol. 'The (Too) Good Soldier: "A Real Story"'. *Glyph*, III (1978), 32–51. On the play of textual and historical inscription in Ford Madox Ford's *The Good Soldier*.

Jameson, Fredric. *The Political Unconscious*. London: Methuen, 1980. Argues for a more politicized approach to the deconstruction of textual gaps and inconsistencies, seen as the 'unconscious' produced by a collision of language, form and ideology. Heavy-going in places, but often persuasive in its effort to negotiate the rift between Marxist and Derridean theories of the text.

Johnson, Barbara. *Défigurations du langage poétique*. Paris: Flammarion, 1979.

Krieger, Murray. 'Poetry Reconstructed'. In his *Theory of Criticism*, 207–45. Baltimore, Md, and London: Johns Hopkins University Press, 1976.

Krieger, Murray. *Poetic Presence and Illusion*. Baltimore, Md, and London: Johns Hopkins University Press, 1979. Looks to Renaissance literary theory, and poets like Sidney, for a parallel with deconstructionist debates over textual 'presence' and 'absence'. Suggests that poems may invoke an imaginary presence (like that of the desired mistress) even where the sense of unattainability is most keenly felt. Underlying Krieger's argument is a constant nostalgic appeal to the 'old' New Critical faith in the poem as a self-possessed structure of meaning.

Leitch, Vincent B. 'The Deconstructive Criticism of J. Hillis Miller' *Critical Inquiry*, VI (1980), 593–607. (See also Miller's reply, 'Theory and Practice', *Critical Inquiry*, VI (1980), 609–14.)

Lentricchia, Frank. *After the New Criticism*. London: Athlone Press, 1980. An ambitious account of American post-structuralist criticism and its main continental sources. Generally favours a 'worldly' or activist rhetoric (Foucault, Said), as opposed to what he sees as the disengaged 'pure' textuality of Derrida's closest disciples. Provocative but scrupulously argued – a valuable work of introduction.

Michaels, Walter Benn. 'Saving the Text: Reference and Belief'. *Modern Language Notes*, XCIII (1978), 771–93.

Miller, J. Hillis. *Thomas Hardy: Distance and Desire*. Cambridge, Mass.: Harvard University Press, 1970.

Miller, J. Hillis. 'The Fiction of Realism: *Sketches by Boz, Oliver Twist*, and Cruikshank's Illustrations'. In Ada Nisbet and Blake Nevius (eds), *Dickens Centennial Essays*. Berkeley, Calif.: University of California, 1971.

Miller, J. Hillis. Critical Introduction to Thomas Hardy, *The Well-Beloved*. London: Macmillan, 1976. Shrewdly latches on to the self-deconstructing elements in this strangest and least 'credible' of all Hardy's fictions.

Miller, J. Hillis. 'Ariadne's Thread: Repetition and the Narrative Line'. *Critical Inquiry*, III (1976), 57–77.

Miller, J. Hillis. 'The Limits of Pluralism, II: The Critic as Host'. *Critical Inquiry*, III (1977), 439–47.

Norris, Christopher. 'Wrestling With Deconstructors'. *Critical Quarterly*, XXII (1980), 57–62.

Norris, Christopher. 'Derrida at Yale: The "Deconstructive Moment" in Modernist Poetics'. *Philosophy and Literature*, IV (1980), 242–56.

Reed, Arden. 'The Debt of Disinterest: Kant's Critique of Music'. *Modern Language Notes*, XCV (1980), 562–84. A deconstructive reading of Kantian aesthetics, taking a cue from Derrida's remarks (in *Of Grammatology*) on Rousseau and the primacy of melody in music. Shows how a differential 'harmony' always obtrudes its disturbing overtones, just as writing invades the privileged realm of speech.

Ryan, Michael. 'The Act'. *Glyph*, II (1977), 64–87. On the rhetoric of deconstruction in Nietzsche's *Ecce Homo*.

Said, Edward. 'The Text as Practice and as Idea'. *Modern Language Notes*, LXXXVIII (1973), 1071–101.

Said, Edward. *Beginnings: Intention and Method*. Baltimore, Md, and London: Johns Hopkins University Press, 1975. An eloquent if rather long-drawn-out testimony to the impact of French post-structuralism on American critical thought. More indebted to Foucault than to Derrida, in whom Said detects and criticizes a strain of 'nihilistic radicality'. Nevertheless a crucial text for understanding the American response to deconstructionist theory.

Sussman, Henry. 'The Deconstructionist as Politician: Melville's *The Confidence-Man*'. *Glyph*, IV (1978), 33–56.

Weber, Samuel. 'Saussure and the Apparition of Language: The Critical Perspective'. *Modern Language Notes*, XCI (1976), 912–38.

White, Hayden. *Tropics of Discourse*. Baltimore, Md, and London: Johns Hopkins University Press, 1978. Mainly concerned with historical narrative and the various tropes and patterning devices employed to make sense of history. See especially the chapters on Foucault and Derrida, the latter representing for White an 'absurdist' extreme of sceptical philosophy.

Revised bibliography
(1986 reprint)

Altizer, Thomas J. *et al. Deconstruction and Theology*. New York: Crossroads, 1982.
Arac, Jonathan *et al. The Yale Critics: Deconstruction in America*. Minneapolis: University of Minnesota Press, 1983.
Atkins, G. Douglas. *Quests of Difference: Reading Pope's Poems*. Lexington, Kentucky: University Press of Kentucky, 1986.
Atkins, G. Douglas. *Reading Deconstruction/Deconstructive Reading*. Lexington: University of Kentucky Press, 1984.
Atkins, G. Douglas and Johnson, Michael L. (eds). *Writing and Reading Differently: Deconstruction and the Teaching of Composition and Literature*. Lawrence, Kansas: University Press of Kansas, 1985.
Bennington, Geoff. 'Reading Allegory' (on de Man's *Allegories of Reading*). *The Oxford Literary Review*, IV (1981), 83–93.
Bloom, Harold. *Agon: Towards a Theory of Revisionism*. London and New York: Oxford University Press, 1982.
Bloom, Harold. *The Breaking of the Vessels*. Chicago, Ill., and London: University of Chicago Press, 1982.
Bruss, Elizabeth. *Beautiful Theories: The Spectacle of Discourse in Contemporary Criticism*. Baltimore, Md: Johns Hopkins University Press, 1982.
Butler, Christopher. *Interpretation, Deconstruction and Ideology*. London: Oxford University Press, 1984.
Carroll, David. *The Subject in Question: The Languages of Theory and the Strategies of Fiction*. Chicago, Ill.: University of Chicago Press, 1982.
Cascardi, A. J. 'Skepticism and Deconstruction'. *Philosophy and Literature*, VIII (1984), 1–14.
Chase, Cynthia. 'Getting Versed: Reading Hegel with Baudelaire'. *Studies in Romanticism*, XXII (1983), 241–66.
Corngold, Stanley. *The Fate of the Self: German Writers and French Theory*. New York: Columbia University Press, 1986.
Culler, Jonathan. 'Convention and Meaning: Derrida and Austin'. *New Literary History*, XIII (1981), 15–30.
Culler, Jonathan. *On Deconstruction: Theory and Criticism after Structuralism*. London: Routledge & Kegan Paul, 1983.
Deleuze, Gilles. *Nietzsche and Philosophy* (trans. Hugh Tomlinson). London: Athlone Press, 1983.
de Man, Paul. 'Pascal's Allegory of Persuasion'. In Stephen Greenblatt (ed.), *Allegory and Representation*. Baltimore, Md: Johns Hopkins University Press, 1981, 1–25.
de Man, Paul. 'The Resistance to Theory'. *Yale French Studies*, 63 (1982), 3–20.

de Man, Paul. 'Hypogram and Inscription: Michael Riffaterre's Poetics'. *Diacritics*, XI (1981), 17–35.

de Man, Paul. Introduction to Hans Robert Jauss, *Toward an Aesthetics of Reception* (trans. Timothy Bahti). Minneapolis: University of Minnesota Press, 1982, vii–xxv.

de Man, Paul. 'Sign and Symbol in Hegel's *Aesthetics*'. *Critical Inquiry*, VIII (1982), 761–75.

de Man, Paul. 'Dialogue and Dialogism'. *Poetics Today*, IV (1983), 99–107.

de Man, Paul. 'Hegel on the Sublime'. In Mark Krupnick (ed.), *Displacement: Derrida and After*. Bloomington, Ind.: Indiana University Press, 1983, 139–53.

de Man, Paul. 'Phenomenality and Materiality in Kant'. In Gary Shapiro and Alan Sica (eds), *Hermeneutics: Questions and Prospects*. Amherst, Ma.: University of Massachusetts Press, 1984, 121–44.

de Man, Paul. *The Rhetoric of Romanticism*. New York: Columbia University Press, 1984.

de Man, Paul. *Blindness and Insight: Essays in the Rhetoric of Contemporary Criticism* (2nd edn, expanded and revised). London: Methuen, 1983.

Derrida, Jacques. 'The Law of Genre'. *Glyph*, VII (1980), 202–29.

Derrida, Jacques. 'Economimesis'. *Diacritics*, XI (1981), 3–25.

Derrida, Jacques. *Dissemination* (trans. Barbara Johnson). London: Athlone Press, 1981.

Derrida, Jacques. 'Title (to be specified)'. *Substance*, 31 (1981), 5–22.

Derrida, Jacques. 'Les Morts de Roland Barthes'. *Poetique*, 47 (1981), 269–92.

Derrida, Jacques. *Margins of Philosophy* (trans. Alan Bass). Chicago, Ill.: University of Chicago Press, 1982.

Derrida, Jacques. Interview with Christie V. MacDonald in *Diacritics*, XII (1982), 66–76.

Derrida, Jacques. *L'Oreille de l'autre: otobiographies, transferts, traductions: textes et débats avec Jacques Derrida* (ed. Claude Lévesque and Christie V. MacDonald). Paris: VLB, 1982.

Derrida, Jacques. 'The Time of a Thesis'. In Alan Montefiore (ed.), *Philosophy in France Today*. Cambridge: Cambridge University Press, 1982.

Derrida, Jacques. 'Mes Chances: Au Rendez-Vous de Quelques Stéréophonies Épicuriennes'. *Tijdschrift Voor Filosofie*, XLV (1983), 3–40.

Derrida, Jacques. 'Devant La Loi'. In A. Phillips Griffiths (ed.), *Philosophy and Literature*. Cambridge: Cambridge University Press, 1984.

Derrida, Jacques. *Signéponge/Signsponge* (trans. Richard Rand). New York: Columbia University Press, 1984.

Derrida, Jacques. 'Of an Apocalyptic Tone Recently Adopted in Philosophy' (trans. John P. Leavey). *The Oxford Literary Review*, VI (1984), 3–37.

Derrida, Jacques. 'An Idea of Flaubert: "Plato's Letter"' (trans. Peter Starr). *Modern Language Notes*, XCIX (1984), 748–68.

Derrida, Jacques. *Feu La Cendre* (French text with Italian translation by Stefano Agosti). Firenze: Sansoni, 1984.

Derrida, Jacques. 'No Apocalypse, Not Now (Seven Missiles, Seven Missives)' (trans. Catherine Porter and Philip Lewis). *Diacritics*, XIV (1984), 20–31.

Detweiler, Robert (ed.). *Derrida and Biblical Studies*. Chico, Cal.: Scholar's Press, 1982.

Eagleton, Terry. *Literary Theory: An Introduction*. Oxford: Blackwell, 1983.

152   Deconstruction: Theory and Practice

Evans, Malcolm. *Signifying Nothing: Truth's True Contents in Shakespeare's Text.* Brighton: Harvester Press, 1986.

Fekete, John. *The Structural Allegory: Reconstructive Encounters with the New French Thought.* Manchester: Manchester University Press, 1984.

Felman, Shoshana (ed.). *Literature and Psychoanalysis: The Question of Reading: Otherwise.* Baltimore, Md: Johns Hopkins University Press, 1982.

Felman, Shoshana. *The Literary Speech-Act: Don Juan with J. L. Austin, or Seduction in Two Languages* (trans. Catherine Porter). Ithaca, NY: Cornell University Press, 1983.

Felperin, Howard. *Beyond Deconstruction: The Uses and Abuses of Literary Theory.* Oxford: Clarendon Press, 1985.

Fischer, Michael. *Does Deconstruction Make Any Difference? Post-structuralism and the Defence of Poetry in Modern Criticism.* Bloomington, Ind.: Indiana University Press, 1985.

Fish, Stanley E. 'With the Compliments of the Author: Reflections on Austin and Derrida'. *Critical Inquiry*, VIII (1982), 693–72.

Flores, Ralph. *The Rhetoric of Doubtful Authority: Deconstructive Readings of Self-Questioning Narratives: St Augustine to Faulkner.* Ithaca, NY: Cornell University Press, 1984.

Flynn, Bernard C. 'Textuality and the Flesh: Derrida and Merleau-Ponty'. *Journal of the British Society for Phenomenology*, XV (1984), 164–79.

Gasché, Rodolphe. *The Tain of the Mirror* (on Derrida's philosophical background: demanding but immensely valuable). Cambridge, Mass.: Harvard University Press, 1986.

Gearhart, Suzanne. 'Philosophy *Before* Literature: Deconstruction, Historicity and the Work of Paul de Man'. *Diacritics*, XIII (winter 1983), 63–81.

Gloversmith, Frank (ed.). *The Theory of Reading.* Brighton: Harvester Press, 1984.

Goodheart, Eugene. *The Skeptic Disposition in Contemporary Criticism.* Princeton, NJ: Princeton University Press, 1985.

Graham, Joseph F. (ed.). *Difference in Translation.* Ithaca, NY: Cornell University Press, 1985.

Halliburton, David. *Poetic Thinking: An Approach to Heidegger.* Chicago, Ill.: University of Chicago Press, 1982.

Handelman, Susan. *The Slayers of Moses: The Emergence of Rabbinic Interpretation in Modern Literary Theory.* Albany, NY: State University of New York Press, 1982.

Hartman, Geoffrey. 'How Creative Should Literary Criticism Be?'. *New York Times Book Review*, 5 April 1981, 11, 24–5.

Hartman, Geoffrey. '"Timely Utterance" Once More'. *Genre*, XVII (1984), 37–49.

Hartman, Geoffrey. *Easy Pieces* (recent essays and review-articles). New York: Columbia University Press, 1985.

Hartman, Geoffrey and Budick, Sanford (eds). *Midrash and Literature.* New Haven, Conn.: Yale University Press, 1986.

Harvey, Irene. *Derrida and the Economy of Differance.* Bloomington, Ind.: Indiana University Press, 1986.

Hertz, Neil. *The End of the Line: Essays on Psychoanalysis and the Sublime.* New York: Columbia University Press, 1985.

Hobson, Marian. 'Scroll-Work' (on Derrida's *La Verité en Peinture*). *Oxford Literary Review*, IV (1981), 94–102.

Hughes, Daniel. 'Geoffrey Hartman, Geoffrey Hartman'. *Modern Language Notes*, XCVI (1981), 1134–48.

Johnson, Barbara. *The Critical Difference: Essays in the Contemporary Rhetoric of Reading*. Baltimore, Md: Johns Hopkins University Press, 1981.

Johnson, Barbara (ed.). *The Pedagogical Imperative* (*Yale French Studies*, 63). New Haven, Conn.: Yale University Press, 1981.

Kermode, Frank. *Essays on Fiction, 1971–82*. London: Routledge & Kegan Paul, 1983.

Kofman, Sarah. *Lectures de Derrida*. Paris: Galilée, 1984.

Krupnick, Mark (ed.). *Displacement: Derrida and After*. Bloomington, Ind.: Indiana University Press, 1983.

Lacoue-Labarthe, Philippe and Nancy, Jean-Luc (eds). *Les Fins de l'homme*. Paris: Galilée, 1981.

Leavey, John P. 'Jacques Derrida's *Glas*: A Translated Selection and Some Comments on an Absent Colossus'. *Clio*, XI (1982), 327–37.

Lecercle, Jean-Jacques. *Philosophy through the Looking-Glass: Language, Nonsense, Desire*. London: Hutchinson, 1985.

Leitch, Vincent. *Deconstructive Criticism: An Advanced Introduction*. New York: Columbia University Press, 1983.

Lentricchia, Frank. *Criticism and Social Change*. Chicago, Ill.: University of Chicago Press, 1983.

Llewelyn, John. *Derrida on the Threshold of Sense* (offers some acute philosophical commentary). London: Macmillan, 1985.

MacCannell, Juliet Flower. 'Portrait: de Man'. *Genre*, XVII (1984), 51–74.

Machin, Richard. *Paul de Man*. London: Croom Helm, forthcoming 1986.

Machin, Richard and Norris, Christopher (eds). *Post-Structuralist Readings of English Poetry*. Cambridge: Cambridge University Press, forthcoming.

Magliola, Robert. *Derrida on the Mend*. West Lafayette, Ind.: Purdue University Press, 1984.

Megill, Alan. *Prophets of Extremity: Nietzsche, Heidegger, Foucault, Derrida*. Berkeley and Los Angeles: University of California Press, 1985.

Melville, Stephen. *Philosophy Beside Itself: On Deconstruction and Modernism*. Minneapolis: University of Minnesota Press, 1986.

Merrell, Floyd. *Deconstruction Reframed*. West Lafayette, Ind.: Purdue University Press, 1985.

Michaels, Walter Benn and Knapp, Steven. 'Against Theory'. *Critical Inquiry*, VIII (1982), 723–42.

Miller, J. Hillis. 'Remembering and Disremembering in Nietzsche's "On Truths and Lies in a Non-Moral Sense"'. *Boundary 2*, IX (1981), 41–54.

Miller, J. Hillis. *Fiction and Repetition: Seven English Novels*. Oxford: Blackwell, 1982.

Miller, J. Hillis. 'The Search for Grounds in Literary Study'. *Genre*, XVII (1984), 19–36.

Miller, J. Hillis. *The Linguistic Moment: Wordsworth to Stevens*. Princeton, NJ: Princeton University Press, 1985.

Miller, J. Hillis. *The Ethics of Reading*. New York: Columbia University Press, 1986.

Middleton, Peter. 'The Revolutionary Poetics of William Blake: Silence, Syntax and Spectres'. *Oxford Literary Review*, VI (1983), 35–51.

Mitchell, Sollace. 'Post-Structuralism, Empiricism and Interpretation'. In Sollace Mitchell and Michael Rosen (eds). *The Need for Interpretation*. London: Athlone Press, 1983, 54–89.

Moi, Toril. *Sexual/Textual Politics: Feminist Literary Theory*. London: Methuen, 1985.

Norris, Christopher. *The Deconstructive Turn: Essays in the Rhetoric of Philosophy*. London: Methuen, 1983.

Norris, Christopher. *The Contest of Faculties: Deconstruction, Philosophy and Theory*. London: Methuen, 1985.

Norris, Christopher. *Jacques Derrida*. London: Fontana, forthcoming 1986.

O'Hara, Daniel T. (ed.). *Why Nietzsche Now?* Bloomington, Ind.: Indiana University Press, 1985.

Parker, Andrew. 'Taking Sides (on History): Derrida re-Marx'. *Diacritics*, XI (1981), 57–73 (review of Lentricchia, *After the New Criticism*).

Pêcheux, Michel. *Language, Semantics and Ideology*. London: Macmillan, 1982.

Rapaport, Herman. 'Geoffrey Hartman and the Spell of Sounds'. *Genre*, XVII (1984), 159–77.

Raval, Suresh. *Metacriticism*. Athens, Georgia: University of Georgia Press, 1981.

Ray, William. *Literary Meaning: From Phenomenology to Deconstruction*. Oxford: Blackwell, 1984.

Reed, Arden (ed.). *Romanticism and Language*. London: Methuen, 1984.

Rorty, Richard. *Consequences of Pragmatism*. Minneapolis: University of Minnesota Press, 1982.

Rorty, Richard. 'Deconstruction and Circumvention'. *Critical Inquiry*, XI (1984), 1–23.

Rose, Gillian. *Dialectic of Nihilism: Post-Structuralism and Law*. Oxford: Blackwell, 1984.

Ryan, Michael. *Marxism and Deconstruction: A Critical Articulation*. Baltimore, Md: Johns Hopkins University Press, 1982.

Said, Edward. *The World, the Text and the Critic*. London: Faber & Faber, 1984.

Schleifer, Ronald. 'The Anxiety of Allegory: de Man, Greimas, and the Problem of Referentiality'. *Genre*, XVII (1984), 215–37.

Scholes, Robert. *Textual Power: Literary Theory and the Teaching of English*. New Haven, Conn.: Yale University Press, 1985.

Selden, Raman. *Criticism and Objectivity*. London: Allen & Unwin, 1984.

Selden, Raman. *A Guide to Modern Literary Theory*. Brighton: Harvester Press, 1985.

Seung, T. K. *Structuralism and Hermeneutics*. New York: Columbia University Press, 1982.

Silverman, Hugh J. and Ihde, Don (eds). *Hermeneutics and Deconstruction*. Albany: State University of New York Press, 1985.

Smith, Joseph H. and Kerrigan, William (eds). *Taking Chances: Derrida, Psychoanalysis and Literature*. Baltimore: Johns Hopkins University Press, 1984.

Spanos, William V. *et al* (eds). *The Question of Textuality: Strategies of Reading in Contemporary Criticism*. Bloomington, Ind.: Indiana University Press, 1982.

Spivak, Gayatri Chakravorty. 'Revolutions that as yet have no Model: Derrida's *Limited Inc.*'. *Diacritics*, X (1980), 29–49.

Spivak, Gayatri Chakravorty. 'Reading the World: Literary Studies in the 1980s'. *College English*, LXIII (1981), 671–9.

Spivak, Gayatri Chakravorty. 'Sex and History in *The Prelude* (1805): Books Nine to Thirteen'. *Texas Studies in Language and Literature*, XXIII (1981), 324–60.

Staten, Henry. *Wittgenstein and Derrida*. Lincoln, Neb. and London: University of Nebraska Press, 1984.

Sussman, Henry. *The Hegelian Aftermath: Readings in Hegel, Kierkegaard, Freud, Proust, and James*. Baltimore, Md: Johns Hopkins University Press, 1982.

Taylor, Mark C. *Erring: A Postmodern A/theology*. Chicago, Ill.: University of Chicago Press, 1984.

Todorov, Tzvetan (ed.). *French Literary Theory Today: A Reader* (trans. R. Carter). Cambridge: Cambridge University Press, 1982.

Tomlinson, Hugh. 'Derrida's Differance (sic)'. *Radical Philosophy*, 25 (1980), 30–3.

Ulmer, Gregory L. *Applied Grammatology: Post(e) Pedagogy from Jacques Derrida to Joseph Beuys*. Baltimore, Md: Johns Hopkins University Press, 1984.

Valdés, Mario J. and Miller, Owen (eds). *The Identity of the Literary Text*. Toronto: University of Toronto Press, 1985.

Weber, Samuel. *The Legend of Freud*. Minneapolis: University of Minnesota Press, 1982.

Wordsworth, Ann. 'Household Words: Alterity, the Unconscious and the Text'. *Oxford Literary Review*, V (1982), 80–95.

Wright, Edmond. 'Derrida, Searle, Contexts, Games, Riddles'. *New Literary History*, XIII (1982), 463–77.

Wright, Elizabeth. *Psychoanalytic Criticism: Theory in Practice*. London: Methuen, 1984.

Wyschogrod, Edith. 'Time and Non-Being in Derrida and Quine'. *Journal of the British Society for Phenomenology*, XIV (1983), 112–26.

Young, Robert (ed.). *Untying the Text: A Post-Structuralist Reader*. London: Routledge & Kegan Paul, 1981.

Young, Robert. 'Post-Structuralism: The End of Theory'. *Oxford Literary Review*, V (1982), 3–20.

The above is a highly selective checklist of books and articles published during the past four years. For a useful survey up to 1980 (including detailed entries on Derrida and de Man), see Richard Barney, 'Deconstructive Criticism: A Selected Bibliography', *SCE Reports*, 8 (1980). Of the books listed above, the following also have extended reference sections: Arac *et al*, The Yale Critics; Bruss, *Beautiful Theories*; Culler, *On Deconstruction*; Eagleton, *Literary Theory*; Leitch, *Deconstructive Criticism*; Ryan, *Marxism and Deconstruction* (on political aspects); and Ulmer, *Applied Grammatology* (on Derrida's latest writings in a broad postmodernist context). Also very welcome are the chapters on 'Literary Theory' contributed by Robert Young to *The Year's Work in English Studies* (1982 and 1983). These provide the best, most authoritative survey of current developments in the field.

Index